DISCERNING YOUR CONGREGATION'S FUTURE

A STRATEGIC AND SPIRITUAL APPROACH

Roy M. Oswald &
Robert E. Friedrich. Jr.

An Alban Institute Publication

Library of Congress Catalog Card 96-85703
ISBN 1-56699-174-9

07   EB   8   9   10   11   12   13   14   15

CONTENTS

PREFACE

It has been said that "if you aim at nothing, you will hit it every time." This is true not only for the corporate boardroom, where the company five-year plan or annual plan or three-month plan has become a standard feature. It is true for the church, where lack of planning is too often the order of the day or the decade.

"Vision" is currently a hot topic in the church. This is good because merely going through the motions of "doing church" is quite obviously unsatisfying and unfruitful. But we are after profound change—the kind that will have to occur in congregations that wish not only to survive but to be spiritually effective into the fast-paced future. Bringing about this kind of change requires clear vision and a plan.

Many congregations are focusing, at least for a moment, on their future life together. In fact, in these waning days of the twentieth century, congregations are more frequently hearing a wake-up call. Their memberships may be declining; their neighborhoods may be changing; their youth may not be coming to worship. Something has alerted them to the fact that from now on "business as usual" will eventually spell death. And something calls them forward—toward a new vision.

This book is for the congregation that wants to stop drifting and to establish a corporate direction. We need to state right up front, however, that this is not yet another book on the need for the *leader* to have and impart a vision to the people. Quite the opposite. We are committed to a theology and methodology that places the entire *congregation* in the center of the visioning process.

This method can also be eminently suited for the work a congregation does in preparing to call a new pastor.

The approach presented in this book is based on recent findings and methods of discerning and planning. Of course, this is not *the* Alban Institute approach. Every consultant will have his or her favorite method, and that is fine. However, we do believe that this procedure provides a unique opportunity for congregations to begin a process of discerning and planning, and fills a gap in the literature on the subject.

Out of the belief that systematic, strategic planning is of immeasurable value in religious congregations—and out of hours of consultation in congregations—have come many of the volumes of research and literature The Alban Institute has produced over the years. This book is an effort to place the means to effect intelligent change in congregations in the hands of the congregational leaders, pastors, and facilitators who work with them.

Using the Behavioral Sciences

The visioning process described in this book was developed by Roy Oswald, a senior consultant with The Alban Institute. Co-author Robert Friedrich is an Episcopal priest who consults with congregations to implement that process. As you get into the heart of the process as we have outlined it, you might well ask why we are using so many behavioral science techniques if our true purpose is to discern the will of God related to our future. That is a fair question. Basically, our perspective is that a congregation needs to know the truth about itself before it can engage in a discernment process. The process of discernment must begin with laying out the facts about the congregation as objectively as possible. The behavioral sciences provide a variety of tools to help determine what the facts are. When the data are available to the whole congregation, the congregation can then enter a discernment process to decide which data are most important to the future, and how they should act on this information.

For example, the chief breadwinner in a family might enter a prayerful discernment process about whether to stay with his or her current job or to take a new job in a new city. Before this person can engage in a discernment process, it is vital that he or she know some basic things about this opportunity, such as how the spouse feels and how the children would manage such a move, what the new job entails, and what the neighborhood and community are like. Although the information gathering process in a congregation will be much more complex than a similar process in a family, it is only when that kind of information is out in the open that a discernment process should begin.

With the planning process we use with congregations, for example, we think it is vital to find out what members value and what things concern them about their congregation. We think it's vital that people reflect openly about the history of the congregation, noting how they are interpreting that history. Of equal importance is their looking honestly at their norms, those unwritten psychological rules that govern behavior within the congregation. In short, it helps to know where a system is hurting before you pray for it to get well.

We also employ some sound behavioral science approaches to human interaction because we believe we need to bring and offer the best we have to God and the church. Over time, behavioral scientists have learned about ways human beings can interact with one another in open and supportive ways. We bring that gift to the church.

A Grassroots Vision

It is not the use of techniques and processes from the behavioral sciences that makes our process unique, however. Rather, the process laid out here will be meaningful to congregations that have a high regard for the *collective wisdom* of their members, guided by God. We, the authors, are convinced that only grassroots visions have any real meaning or staying power. Clergy who go Moses-like up the mountain and return with a revelation can easily mistake their wishes for the Spirit and lead groups hungry for direction down unfruitful, perhaps dangerous, paths. Just as use of the hierarchical model is gradually diminishing in the corporate world, we in the church need a more engaging process for our members if we hope to help them embrace a new future together.

Arriving at a grassroots vision is harder than imposing a vision from above. That is why you can plan to spend six to twelve months on this process. And that is why you will ask the whole congregation to be in active prayer for the congregation throughout this time. Frankly, it would be simpler just to ask the pastor—or rector or vicar or rabbi—to come up with a plan, or to send the board away on a retreat to come back with a hastily concocted "mission statement." But we are dedicating this book to those who want to put effort into something harder, more substantial, and more workable—and something that will pay rich dividends in meaningful planning and congregational investment in the plan.

Discernment, Theology, and Prayer

This book is based on the premise that all of us are in a relationship with a God who is ever more ready to communicate with us than we are to listen, a God who is ever more ready to bestow grace on us than we are to receive it. This God is also willing to offer us direction and perspective if and when we are ready to surrender our willfulness and be open to receiving such direction.

When we say our God is ever more ready to communicate with us than we are to listen, we also need to say that God will rarely overwhelm us with a message so clear and blatant that our freedom to choose is eliminated. God created us with a free will. We will always have the option of either rejecting God or accepting God's invitation to servanthood. Hence, we will rarely experience God speaking to us in such a clear, loud voice that there is no mistaking that this is God's voice and that God wants us to do such and such. From time to time, we will feel a gentle nudge moving us in a certain direction, or we may feel God wooing us to consider coming home. Occasionally we will feel a presence that is almost palpable, yet when reflecting on it later we might wonder whether it was merely our imaginations. Sometimes we might feel God within us, coaching us to yearn for God. And like Elijah we might occasionally hear God talking to us in the "still small voice."

These mystical experiences are certainly not the only way we will come to know God because God will speak to us through Scripture, tradition, community, relationships, and events and experiences. What is needed in all cases is the gift of discernment so we are able to distinguish between messages from God and messages that stem from our own willfulness, our ego, or even our shadow. At all times we need to be aware of the fact that we will always be tempted to think we have a "word from the Lord," when in fact the word comes from our desire, our hubris, our dark side, or the shadow side of other people and community.

There is a saying that when we are in great difficulty or turmoil, the presence and suggested way of the evil one will always appear to us first as an angel of light. In our desperation we will see the easy way out as a message from God. The need to distinguish between messages from God and other messages shows us the importance of the gift of discernment and the importance of always testing our options with a community of faith. Not only do individual Christians need to be connected to a community, but communities of faith need to be connected with other congregations to establish a built-in source of guidance and correction.

A Theology of Discernment

At the very heart of the Christian faith lies one fundamental question: How can we understand and live the will of God?

When Jesus sought a way to identify who was of the family of God, he determined that a member of the family is whoever does the will of God (Mark 3:35). And when he was in agony in the garden of Gethsemane on the night of his betrayal, his prayer was simply and profoundly that God's will be done (Mark 14:35). This desire, this longing to seek to do God's will, is "discernment" and is a hallmark of the Christian faith.

The ongoing presence of Christ in the church and in his followers is manifest in the Holy Spirit. The witness of the apostolic church is that just as the Holy Spirit came upon Jesus in his baptism (Luke 3:21), so with Jesus' resurrection the Holy Spirit is poured out upon his followers that they may witness to the ends of the earth (Acts 1:5,8). For St. Paul, the Spirit is the presence of Christ in and among his people (1 Cor. 6:17, Eph. 2:22). In Johannine understanding, those in Christ are born anew in the Spirit (John 3:5), and this Counselor will guide them into all truth by mediating Christ to believers (John 16:13-15). The church, then, is the community of Christ gathered and led by the Holy Spirit. This is both the apostolic and the Reformation witness to what God intends.

No one person knows fully the will of God. In our sin and finitude, we are not able fully to comprehend or to accomplish God's will. Yet, reconciled to God in Christ and led by the Holy Spirit, we participate in God's own being and will. We trust that when we are faithful and open,

God's will is disclosed to us that we may follow. (God does sometimes make God's will known to people who aren't faithful, who don't care what God wants, but that is another story.) No one person can discern the will of God, but each of us can glimpse an understanding of what God desires. By sharing these understandings in the community of faith, we can enable the wisdom and way of God to emerge among us. Through prayerful reflection and empathic sharing, we can let the Spirit move within us and among us to build a consensus about what is the will of God.

In our sinfulness, we can never be assured that we have truly and fully comprehended God's will, let alone acted on it. But we can trust that the Holy Spirit will lead. Thus, a discernment process should never be seen as closed. In faithfulness, we make and act on decisions for the service of God, but we are ever open to God's further guidance.

Gladly we accept the cost of discipleship, and joyfully we strive to follow in God's will and way. Truly, it is our duty, privilege, and fulfillment as followers of Christ to strive to live the will of God in the grace and power of the Holy Spirit.

The Prophetic Voice and Discernment

Corporate discernment is, in almost every case, more reliable than individual discernment. The exceptions are those times when God requires an individual to be a prophetic voice to God's people, or the voice of conscience to an irreverent community—a community that is pursuing comfort over discipleship, seeking solace and peace when there is no peace, avoiding action when deeds of justice and mercy are called for. In such cases, the voice of the community is *not* more reliable than the individual's. Even in such cases, however, individuals who believe they have been called to be prophetic voices need to test what they discern as God speaking a prophetic word through them with at least one other person who is judged to be a child and servant of God, a person faithful in prayer and scripture reading.

Unless you perceive and have confirmed that God is calling you as an individual to be a prophetic voice to a faltering community, as you begin to think about engaging in a discernment process, we encourage you to invite all your members to engage in the adventure with you. You

are trying to perceive God's call to you as members of the body of
Christ, a people desiring nothing less than to obey God's desire for you
as a community of faith.

Prayer and Discernment

The etymological basis of the term *discernment* comes from the Greek
word that means "to sift through." Very early it was seen as sifting the
wheat from the chaff, sifting through our own interior experiences, ideas,
thoughts, and feelings, all of which are brought about by the circumstances we are in.

It is simply impossible to do spiritual discernment if we do not pray,
that is, consciously seek to find God. Prayer is making myself present to
God within me and around me. We are not aware that God is present to
us unless we focus our awareness on God. We pray in order to become
open to God. And when we bring an openness, a freedom, to our prayer
time, then we are able to adopt the unconditional attitude, "God, when
you show me a direction to follow, I will say 'yes' no matter what the
cost."

Discernment is not simply having the pastor offer a prayer and then
going about working out a solution using the best of our rational skills.
Discernment does not mean we simply go along with the prayer—because that is what we are supposed to do—and then we get down to the
real work of deciding through rational discourse. Discernment means just
the opposite. Our real work is in the praying prior to our board work,
with the rest of the meeting flowing out of that. What follows prayer is
not so much a reasoned approach to things as a genuine listening to one
another, being open to a solution to an issue that is not very rational but
that instead just feels right to the entire group present.

There is nothing rational or prudent about the Paschal Mystery, the
sacrificial life and death of Christ. It is a stumbling block to some and
folly to others, yet it remains the heart of the Good News. Either we believe that, or we are not Christians at all. As we try to discern the will of
God for our congregation, our focus will not be on doing the rational,
prudent thing but rather on doing the faithful thing. In short, when a
Christian congregation tries to discern the will of God for its future, it
most likely will be choosing to continue in the path of Christ—of entering
suffering and brokenness in order to do the sacrificial, life-giving thing.

Prayer and Fasting

Most Christians have lost the spiritual discipline of both fasting and prayer, although every major religion has a tradition of fasting and prayer. When it comes down to the crunch time, however, when your governing board, strategic planning task force, and whoever else participates in choosing your top priorities for the next four years from among fifteen to twenty-five possible options, we encourage as many people as possible to enter into a time of prayer and fasting. There will likely be no clearer signal to your entire congregation that you are engaged in a serious discernment process than when you call for a time of both fasting and prayer. And the discernment process itself provides an opportunity to teach your people this ancient spiritual discipline of combining fasting with prayer.

Appendix A of this book provides guidelines for fasting. Those who feel called to participate need to show up at the church for several hours to receive some guidelines for fasting. We encourage you to make the fast last for a three- to five-day period. Longer fasts are easier and more beneficial than one-day fasts.

Have people gather, for example, from 4:00 P.M. to 6:00 P.M. on a given day. Enumerate and discuss the guidelines for fasting. Invite everyone present to covenant to fast until a specific time and date, when the whole group will meet again to share their experiences and break the fast in silence by eating a piece of fruit. People are encouraged both to journal and to pray throughout this time. The fast is dedicated to discerning God's will for the future of your congregation. Special prayers are made for those carrying the burden of making tough decisions. The decision makers themselves are invited both to fast and to pray during this time.

Scripture suggests that a special power is available when people both fast and pray (Luke 2:37; Acts 13:1-3; 14:23). A kind of clarity is present while fasting. When we are eating regularly, the blood goes from our heads to our stomachs, and our prayers have a kind of sleepiness to them. When we fast, every time we feel a hunger pang we are directed to ask, What am I really hungry for? What is the nature of my deeper spiritual hunger? Our hunger also reminds us that we as a congregation are entering a dangerous "opportunity" (from the Chinese word for "crisis") and that we need to be more diligent in our prayers at this time.

Those burdened with making decisions on behalf of the congregation

are also reminded by their hunger that members of the congregation have
entered a period of intense reflection for the sake of the future health of
the congregation. This thought encourages them to be more diligent in
their own prayers, so that they will make decisions congruent with the
will of God for their congregation. Fasting then is seen as an aid in the
discernment process. Discerning the will of God can often require some
hard work and sacrifices on our part.

New Prayer Forms

In addition to learning something about fasting and prayer in this planning process, we are also invited to engage in different forms of prayer.
If the only types of prayer we are used to are those involving petition and
thanksgiving, we likely have not learned the prayer forms that invite us
to listen to God, overagainst talking to God. The two Greek words that
define these two different forms of prayer are "kataphatic" prayer and
"apophatic" prayer.

Protestant prayer forms in this country are mainly kataphatic prayers
growing out of the Roman school of prayer. This is an active prayer form
in which we approach God with words, concepts, and images. The Alex-
andrian school of prayer, on the other hand, engaged the apophatic prayer form, which taught people how to listen to God. The mystics, for example, felt they could never really contain God in words or images, so
they simply tried to quiet both body and mind to be open to experiencing
the presence of God and to perceiving God's will for them.

Another name for apophatic prayer is contemplative prayer. Others
might call it meditation. When we are not used to this form of praying or
have not been taught how to do it, we can easily become confused and
discouraged. It requires some discipline to stay with the practice of setting aside short periods of time, five to twenty minutes, when we do
nothing but remain quiet and pay attention to everything present to us at
that moment, including God.

Even though the present moment is all that any of us have, we never
feel it is quite enough. We are always tempted to embellish it with
thoughts of the future or the past. This is where the use of a sacred word
or phrase or simple chant can be an aid. The word, phrase, or chant reminds us of God and helps us to stay focused on God. Leading a group in

a prolonged, simple chant can be an effective way of engaging them in a discernment process. A simple refrain sung over and over can keep us centered on God and on the task of discerning God's will for us at this time.

Following five to fifteen minutes of such a chant and a brief period of silence, people can be paired and asked to share any thoughts or insights that came to them during that prayer period. Such a practice is another way of staying open and listening to God. (There are many helpful books and audiocassettes available to teach us about contemplative prayer. An adult seminar in your church on meditation or contemplative prayer can be a helpful prelude to a congregational discernment process.)

Actually, these two forms of prayer—kataphatic and apophatic prayer—form a polarity. Stated simply, a polarity is an unsolvable yet unavoidable problem that needs to be managed. Our only choice is to either manage it well or manage it poorly. Polarities involve two interlocking poles, each with both a positive side and a negative side. You know you are dealing with a polarity when the problem presented by the negative side of one pole is resolved by the positive side of the opposite pole. Let's examine these two forms of prayer as a polarity.

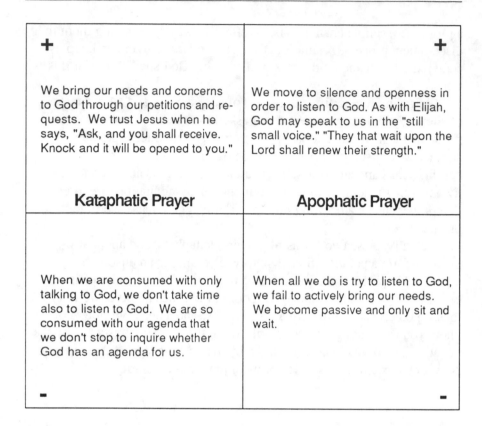

+	+
We bring our needs and concerns to God through our petitions and requests. We trust Jesus when he says, "Ask, and you shall receive. Knock and it will be opened to you."	We move to silence and openness in order to listen to God. As with Elijah, God may speak to us in the "still small voice." "They that wait upon the Lord shall renew their strength."
Kataphatic Prayer	**Apophatic Prayer**
When we are consumed with only talking to God, we don't take time also to listen to God. We are so consumed with our agenda that we don't stop to inquire whether God has an agenda for us.	When all we do is try to listen to God, we fail to actively bring our needs. We become passive and only sit and wait.
–	–

Managing this polarity well would mean finding a healthy balance between the upper two quadrants of this polarity, deepening our capacity for both kinds of prayer. The process of discernment is aided when people are comfortable with both forms of prayer.

Guiding Principles for Discernment

Discerning the will of God in church systems is an essential step in the planning process. This is a relatively new idea in church systems permeated by more secular organizational concepts. Because using discernment as an approach to planning will likely be novel for most clergy and lay leaders, the concept may need some attention. Some sound biblical and theological reflection may be needed before the practice is explored.

Much more could be said about the nature of prayer and the role of various types of prayer in the discernment process. But colleague and friend Bernie Zerkel, formerly a regional executive for the United Church of Christ and now a spiritual guide, has helped develop five principles that outline the connections between God, prayer, and the corporate discernment process.

1. Discernment is a part of the total planning process and cannot be achieved without careful, prayerful attention to seeking the will of God for us as a congregation. Whether the congregation is identifying needs or developing strategic action plans, discernment should be evident in frequent times of reflective prayer.

2. Discernment should be conceived of as part of an ongoing effort of a congregation to determine how God may view the mission of the system.

3. Discernment requires that people understand the church is called to be an effective "servant church" rather than successful church institution.

4. Discernment involves thinking/praying/assessing through alternatives a congregation may be facing.

5. Discernment takes time and cannot be hurried. When it is hurried, it is likely because those in leadership roles have already made up their minds about a solution and want a quick process to sanctify their position.

CHAPTER 1

Before You Begin

There is nothing more potent than a group of people who hold a vision in common. No matter what you do, you cannot sidetrack them. When one of the members begins to doubt the vision, the others quickly bring this person back in line. Their focus tends to center their corporate energy only on those things that will move them toward their goal.

One example of how a common vision can transform a community of people is what happened several years ago to the people who made Chevrolet trucks. When the company developed a new advertizing campaign and the song "Like a Rock" started to hit the airwaves, the song's impact was felt not only by potential customers but by the workers, on whom it had an even greater impact. Workers felt they had to live up to the image set for them in that advertizing blitz. This incident is a powerful reminder of the impact a mission statement can have on a group of people.

Some visions are demonic. And yet because they are shared by many people, they are so powerful that it takes the combined forces of many nations to bring them to a halt. The Nazi movement in Germany had a common vision of a superior race that would dominate the world. Once the throngs bought into Hitler's vision, there was no stopping them. It required some heroic efforts on the part of all the Allies to stop the movement of this demonic, common vision.

Returning to a positive note, people involved in church growth are aware that it is often easier to start a new church and grow it into a program- or corporate-size church than to begin with an existing congregation, even in a growing area, and help it grow. (This is not true in every circumstance, of course. Exceptional, well-established congregations are able to grow along with their neighborhoods, but they are few and far between.)

We, the authors, believe it is easier to grow a new church because of the vision thing. Starting a new congregation carries with it the excitement of creating something new, yet none of the dreams will ever materialize unless the new congregation grows in size. The vision held in common by all the members of the new mission is a vision of what the congregation might be when it grows. The members continually go out of their way to invite their friends and neighbors to church. Their hopes and dreams for the future depend on their remaining steadfast in this vision, while the vision itself provides much of the motivation to bring about its own fulfillment.

The Framework

This book about helping a congregation develop a common vision began with a theology of discernment because the work of strategic planning in the church is at heart about our relationship with God. Planning for ministry, therefore, is a spiritual discernment process. Businesses regularly engage in strategic planning in order to refine their ability to meet customer needs. Correspondingly, the "business" of the religious congregation is to market its unchanging product—the Good News—to people who live in a changing environment. The congregation asks the question, What does God want us to do and be in this place at this time in history?

Three assumptions about the discernment process are at work in this book. First, the best plan for an individual congregation is one developed by that congregation's own members. When the members and leaders are involved from start to finish, both members and leaders will be able to embrace the result and put it to work.

Second, while this design involves examining psychological and sociological data, a corporate spirituality is also at work in this process. As the people assembled assess their ministry, their norms, and the needs of their community, and derive from that assessment specific ministry goals, they are engaging in a type of spiritual interaction that engages both individuals and the community in discerning God's plan for the assembly.

Every congregation that tries to discern its future needs to consider several basic spiritual issues.

- In this congregation, in what ways are we becoming more faithful to the life and teachings of Christ?
- How well are we making disciples out of our members?
- In what ways are we good stewards of the gifts and resources available to this congregation?
- How is what we are about as a congregation related to Kingdom issues, rather than to keeping an institution alive?
- In what ways do we make room for the Spirit continually to revitalize and refocus our congregation?

These spiritual issues need to be addressed with compassion if yours is to be a faithful and effective community of faith in your neighborhood.

Third, a systems approach to the work of the congregation is a singularly helpful way to understand congregational dynamics. A congregation is a system, much like the interconnected, fragile ecosystems in parts of the environment. For example, when a congregation shifts the Boy Scouts meeting to Wednesday evening, their noise upsets the choir director, who becomes irritable with the choir, which causes one member to complain to the pastor, who raises the issue at the next board meeting, which ends in some regrettable words being said, which affects the morale of the entire congregation. (If you wish to explore this approach further, refer to the resources listed at the end of the chapter.)

The Size of Your Congregation

The importance of a congregation's size cannot be underestimated, and one of the first questions congregations considering taking on strategic planning ask is, Is my church too big (or too small) to do this 'right'? The answer is, of course, there is no "right" way to do strategic planning. Each of the chapters in this book follows a simple outline of three questions:

- What needs to happen?
- Why should it happen?
- How might it be done?

At times suggestions will be made for ways to adapt specific activities for groups of various sizes. Use these suggestions as models to help you modify other activities. In general, you are encouraged to take the philosophy at work (stated right up front in each chapter) and to adapt the suggested means to suit your own situation.

Congregations of all sizes—family, pastoral, program, and corporate—have been able to adapt this program with great success. To be sure, accommodations must be made. For instance, in a large corporate church, Ladue Chapel Presbyterian Church in St. Louis, Missouri, the church office assisted in mobilizing a system that allowed hundreds of parishioners to sign up for and take part in over thirty fireside groups for ministry assessment. On the other hand, a pastoral-size church (which has been family size most of its life), the Episcopal Church of the Epiphany in Newport, New Hampshire, mobilized five groups for the same purpose, and each group was led by a member of the strategic planning task force. So you can plan to be creative and proceed with confidence that this process will work for your congregation!

Preparing the Congregation

As a prelude to helping a congregation develop a common vision, the congregation needs to learn about the nature and process of discernment. You might plan a series of sermons on individual and corporate discernment. Another option would be to offer a six-week seminar on discernment. Invite people to bring to God in prayer their questions about their next steps in life and teach them ways to listen and discern where God is calling them. Also examine the role of discernment in the faith community as a whole.

At the same time as the entire congregation is learning about discernment, you will want to engage your governing board in a time of prayerful listening about whether or not they perceive that they and the congregation are ready for such a corporate discernment process. The discernment and planning process we are suggesting calls for at least four congregationwide meetings over the course of six to twelve months. Congregational leaders need to ask whether the congregation is ready spiritually to take on this kind of prayerful process.

Communicate with your board as clearly as possible the fact that the congregation is entering a time of great vulnerability and possibly a

major shift in direction, and that everyone in the congregation is expected to be in prayer about this for the next six to twelve months. Invite
members of your board to be in prayer themselves over the course of
several months to ascertain whether the timing is right and whether the
congregation is ready for such a major intervention into its corporate life.
(*Transforming Church Boards* by Chuck Olsen, discussed below, is a
useful tool for helping leaders learn the discernment process themselves,
so that they are able in turn to discern the congregation's readiness for a
planning process.)

There should be an atmosphere of excitement and anticipation
among board members about this. Indicate to your board that one of the
key learnings you expect to come out of this process is what you as a
congregation will learn about individual and corporate discernment. The
end result may be that it will radically change the way all future decisions are made in the congregation.

Transforming Your Board

An excellent book for your governing board to read and discuss in preparation for this process is Chuck Olsen's book, *Transforming Church
Boards*, an Alban publication. Transforming the way your governing
board goes about making decisions is an excellent first step in moving
your congregation deeply into using corporate discernment as a way to
make all basic decisions related to congregational life.

Olsen has some wonderful suggestions about how to help your
governing board give up basically corporate world decision-making
processes to begin doing "worshipful work." Rather than burning themselves out with endless debate about important decisions, people serving
a congregational board who fashion their meetings after Olsen's suggestions sing, pray, make confession, receive absolution, and observe periods of silence for discernment. Such actions are the heart of a board
meeting. People go home after such meetings refreshed, rather than
exhausted and unable to sleep because they are so keyed up. They feel
refreshed because they have been through an experience of spiritual
renewal.

Defining Discernment

Olsen helpfully leads into his description of "worshipful work" by out-
lining what discernment is and what it is not.

Discernment Is Not

Discernment is not to be equated with consensus decision making.
We welcome the new openness that the consensus process brings,
with more participation in, ownership of, and the commitment to the
decisions made. Consensus beats the win-lose approach that can
polarize and divide. But Jesus was crucified at the end of a consensus
decision. Humanity's reasoned judgments have limitations and can
easily go astray. My Calvinist tradition teaches that humankind's
capacity for self-deception is limitless.

Discernment is not a political process. . .

Discernment is not a logical, rational, ordered discipline that leads
deductively to inescapable conclusions. . .

Discernment is not to be equated with making decisions. . .

Discernment Is

Discernment means to "see" or to "know" or to "acknowledge" what
is. It is to see the movement of God, perhaps only in the dust kicked
up by the wind. It is to see from God's perspective. If this is so, then
the discernment process is one of uncovering the decision—not of
making it. The Spirit prays within us "with sighs too deep for
words." As we listen to the Spirit, those prayers begin to surface into
our consciousness. They may have been operating subliminally, like
popcorn ads that can be flashed too fast for the human eye to detect
in a movie theater but yield a craving for popcorn.[1]

Commendations for Congregations

Olsen also makes the following commendations for those choosing to use a discernment process in congregational decision making.

Be selective in the number of issues to be discerned. Thinking in terms of an annual agenda, that may mean only several significant decisions over the course of a year—and certainly not more than one per meeting.

Begin with corporate and private self-surrender. Surrender, especially of the ego, is hard to do. We tend to hold on to our pet investments and our pride. "Not my will, but thine be done" is a corporate issue that rarely gets named. Jesus said, "Unless a grain of wheat falls to the earth and dies, it remains just a single grain; but if it dies, it bears much fruit" (John 12:24). Take time to name what needs to die before the discernment begins. . . . Tilden Edwards of the Shalem Institute observes that a deliberative debate or discussion that has gone on for longer than twenty minutes will be ego driven. He suggests stopping the discussion for two minutes to refocus.

One test of readiness for corporate discernment is to ask if there is truly willingness and readiness to follow whatever leading may come.

Focus on core, scripture-based values and beliefs.

Gather information from many quarters and listen to one another.

Allow time in silence both at and between meetings for prayer and deep listening.

Come to agreement on what your common prayer will be. Jesus said, "If two of you agree on earth about anything you ask, it will be done for you by my Father in heaven" (Matt. 18:19). One of the boards with which we were working used the saying, "We are forming our prayer." They meant that they were agreeing on what their prayer would be—asking for what was beyond their reach. This became a prelude to making a policy or program decision.

Seek consensus in the decision. . .

Trust God's power to accomplish God's will and offer it back to us as a gift. It may take more than human effort to bring a vision to reality. There is more for which to pray. The final outcome and shape may not yet be visible.

Recognize that some members of the council may have special gifts of "distinguishing among spirits." Their wisdom will be invaluable, modeling a gift that can be cultivated in other members of the group.[2]

Your Own Discernment

So far you have read about some basic principles and guidelines about what discernment is and is not, and how to make the process work well. It is still not time to begin, though. First, take some time to discern your own sense about why your congregation needs a process like this now in its life. Probe deeply your underlying motivation for wanting a discernment process for your congregation, as well as your sense about why this might be beneficial for your congregation. Allow the discernment process to begin immediately, before you try to understand all the "how tos" of this planning process.

Take time now to enter silence and become reacquainted with some of your own personal spiritual needs. What is your soul lacking right now? What is your own spiritual hunger that you wish your congregation could address? What are some of your key concerns about your congregation as you try to project what its future will be like, even during the next five years? Do you think your congregation is ready to take on the spiritual disciplines required in such a discernment process? What indicators do you see that your people are ready for something new and exciting? What indicators tell you they like things just exactly as they are now?

To what extent can you sense God calling you to introduce a discernment process to your congregation? Can you sell them on the need for a strategic plan for the next four to five years and then engage them in as much of the spiritual discernment part as they can handle? (Remember,

Jesus advised his disciples to be wise as serpents and gentle as doves.) Are you ready to live with the end results of a discernment process?

Will you be able to guide others later through the process of discerning for themselves their own answers to the questions you are asking now?

Take some time now to discern where you are regarding such a planning process.

The Method

If you decide after a period of personal discernment to engage with your congregation in a strategic planning process using this book, you will be encouraged to engage in a discernment process all along the way. At each stage you will be given options about how to proceed. Be in prayer about which options in the book best suit the readiness and needs of your people.

The core of the process described in this book is as follows:

- Appoint a task force
- Assess the congregation's ministry
- Reflect on the congregation's history
- Identify the congregation's norms
- Interview key people in the community
- (Optional) Survey the congregation to evaluate data gathered
- Prioritize the goals
- Share these priorities at a congregational meeting
- Hold a governing board retreat
- Develop a mission statement

Because congregational life is often more complex than normally meets the eye, you are provided with a bundle of designs, instruments, exercises, activities, and the like that will help you handle some of that complexity in order to move toward an exciting, dynamic future. You do not need to implement every suggestion made in this book, but at each step alternative approaches are provided. What this book describes is basically a spiritual discernment process, and there is no set formula for

engaging a congregation in such a process. You do, however, need to
pray lots and listen lots.

Whole-Congregation Events

Do not short circuit any of the discernment activities, particularly the
whole-congregation events. These are activities designed to engage your
entire congregation, or at least the members motivated to participate, in
the discernment process. You need the participation of as many people as
possible in order to get a good fix on various aspects of your faith community.

In many ways a congregation is like a family. Each child in a family
has his or her own perceptions about what family life was like when they
were growing up. When children get together and discuss growing up in
the family, inevitably they gain insight from one another into the family's
dynamics. Yet no insight would be as accurate as when the entire family,
under the guidance of an outside facilitator, reflects on the family's life.
Individual family members can gain a perspective on family life that
would not be possible if the entire family did not share its perceptions.

In like manner, every member of your congregation has a different
fix on the strengths of the congregation, its weaknesses, and some activities that might help the congregation to flourish. Engaging members
in a process of reflection not only helps members gain a more accurate
picture of your congregation but also engages people in working together
to resolve difficulties and challenges and to build on strengths.

Spiritual Reflection

Because congregational discernment is at base a spiritual activity and not
just another planning process, begin every meeting in this process with
some sort of centering, meditation, reading, group reflection, or Scripture
study, and individual and corporate prayer. You will find two options
here: centering prayer and a meditation on Scripture. Yet you ought to
feel free to skip what we recommend and move to a spiritual reflection
activity that you feel is more relevant to the group gathered or to what
has just taken place in your community.

Let no meeting begin, however, without spiritual nourishment of some sort. Do not give way to the temptation to skip over the personal growth time in order to get down to business. These times help people make the transition from their daily life activities to the spiritual business of the session, and spiritual nourishment pays rich dividends in the increased ability of participants to focus on the job at hand. At the end of the entire process, you want the people who were most heavily engaged to feel that the entire process was spiritually uplifting to them.

Team Building

Related to this need for spiritual reflection is a similar need for community building. Find some way for the people gathered to connect as a human community before you dive into the issues at hand. Many people volunteer to serve on a task force such as this simply because they want to be more fully connected with other people in the congregation. So in addition to some prayer and reflection time, allow at least ten to fifteen minutes for people to share with one another the high and low points of their days, their reflections on a congregational incident, or simply their sense of the state of their soul on this particular evening. At the end of this visioning process, you want people to be saying to themselves, "Wow! That sure was a neat group of people I was privileged to work with over these past few months."

Closing Critique

Finally, let no meeting connected with this planning process end without five or ten minutes of reflection about how people felt they worked together to complete the task at hand. At the top of Alban researchers' list of the things that contribute most to lay leader burnout is atrocious meetings. What we make people endure during the course of a meeting is often brutal. People labor for hours, go home exhausted and needing to go to work the next day, and wonder what that was all about.

We have discovered that the quality of meetings tends to rise in direct proportion to the time given after each meeting to reflection on group process. When at times people share their frustration that parts of

the meeting were a waste of time, whoever was chairing the meeting that
evening may receive a barb or two, but that chairperson is likely to manage subsequent gatherings more efficiently. A period of critique at the
end of each congregational meeting seems to result in meetings that are
shorter yet more satisfying.

Some Words of Caution

At the beginning of this chapter, you read about the power of a vision
held in common by members of a group. In a congregation that has been
around for twenty to eighty years or more, that common vision is long
gone. What usually takes its place is the dream that they might serve
their own members more fully. Now instead of the vision being directed
outward to mission and engagement with the neighborhood, it is focused
inward on serving existing members. The people may voice their desire
to grow numerically, but all of their energy tends to be focused on serving their own needs more fully.

Additionally, an older congregation's members hold quite disparate
views about what the mission of the congregation ought to be. Rather
than holding a vision in common, they learn to live with each other, even
though they have great difficulty agreeing on where the congregation
ought to focus its energy.

As you consider taking your congregation into a discernment and
visioning process, you need to be aware how incredibly difficult it is
going to be to really get the majority of the members to agree on a common set of goals and objectives. Discerning the will of God for your
congregation takes time and the prayerful involvement of as many of
your people as possible. What God may be calling you to be or do as a
congregation may require a radical departure from the way your congregation is currently functioning. This, of necessity, is going to upset some
of your people in no small way.

Your congregation is going to have to pay a price for engaging in an
exciting new vision. Some people likely will decide to leave the congregation as you head in a new direction. You may end up with the majority
of your people giving a tacit nod of approval to a specific set of goals,
but you need to recognize that this approval is quite different from that
given by a group of people on fire about a sense of mission they hold in
common.

The lack of agreement among members will be anxiety provoking for your strategic planning task force and your governing board. In addition, if your decision makers are not convinced the congregation is engaging in a deeply grounded, spiritual process, they will inevitably decide to move in the easiest, safest, least offensive path possible. When this happens, it is unlikely that an exciting new vision for the congregation is going to emerge. Your decision makers will be listening to voices of political prudence rather than listening to a God who calls us to radical discipleship in a changing, uncertain world. Everyone needs to be in prayer as you face a variety of tough challenges.

Some Words of Encouragement

It is because some people will always resist change that we have built into the process opportunity for heavy involvement from the entire congregation. The more members become engaged in the planning process, the more they will feel ownership of the final goals. Yet this is where the process becomes dicey. When the majority of members only think in self-serving terms, where will the vision for a more outward mission come from?

It is here that using a dialogical process really pays off. To be sure, everyone needs to feel like they have gained something important to them in the final goals and objectives. Yet by setting up occasions when members can talk with each other about what they feel God wants them to do and be for the next few years, those who have more of a sense of mission and outreach can bring others into that vision. A dialogical process does make it possible for a broad representation of members within your congregation to come to some agreement about a possible new vision for the congregation.

It is here that years of solid preaching and prayer and the study of Scripture begins to pay off. It is through this type of steady spiritual nurture that people are brought to the place where they have a common understanding of what it really means to be a faithful member of the body of Christ, or a faithful practicing Jew.

Factors That Support Change

In fact, when three important factors converge within a congregation's life, positive change is much more likely to occur. These factors are like three interlocking circles.

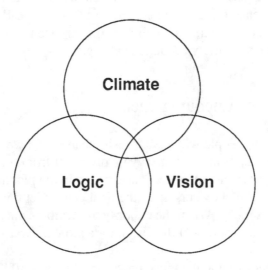

Climate has to do with a general sense of warmth and good feeling members have towards each other. It also has to do with your congregation being a friendly, welcoming place for outsiders. Any congregation can benefit from building closer networks of relationships within the congregation. This is one clear reason for engaging members in team building before every committee or group meeting. Behavioral scientists have documented that the quality of decision making on any committee tends to rise when the group begins a meeting by connecting on a human level first. This usually involves taking ten to fifteen minutes at the start of a committee meeting for an activity like having everyone share the high and low points of their days, or having them talk about where they saw God's presence in some act of compassion that day, as well as where they encountered the demonic.

　　Climate is the reason for having the occasional potluck dinner, a coffee hour following services, or progressive dinners. It is also the reason for teaching good conflict resolution skills to members, so the congregation can manage differences in constructive ways.

For some people, you can never do enough work on climate. It is their favorite issue, and they believe all the problems of the congregation would go away if only people got to know each other more deeply. Yet other components to congregational life need attention.

Logic may seem like a strange word to define this aspect of congregational life, but it basically refers to a common understanding in a group about what it means to be a faithful member. It is here that our understanding of Scripture and theology becomes important. You might say this is the disciple-making task of every congregation. To what extent are your members grounded in the basics of the faith?

Building logic also is a never ending task. When people go church shopping, they are looking for the congregation that will offer them the most of what they are seeking in a community of faith. This often centers on serving "me" best. Does this Presbyterian congregation down the street have as much to offer as the Methodist congregation across town? The church's task is to take people who come in looking to be served and turn them into servant people.

Now if you don't think that is a challenge, think again. People may come in searching for ways to fill their spiritual hunger, but they usually have a hard time accepting the fact that they will need to face their dark, shadow side and admit they fall far short of God's standards for human life. Changing someone from a self-centered, grasping individual into a grateful, joyful, giving person is no easy task. Yet it is when we have some common understanding that this is what God wants for us that we have some agreement about the logic of the faith.

Just as some people think congregational life is all about climate, others think the congregation never does enough related to logic. The church never has enough Bible studies or forums where people can discuss theology to suit them.

Vision is our common understanding of where we believe God wants us to go in the future. This book is about creating a vision by using a process we've developed that will help you reach consensus about six to eight broad goals for the congregation over the next four years, plus some strategies about how to accomplish these goals. Yet unless this vision is undergirded by both logic and climate, it will likely not amount to much.

As with the other two factors, there are people who think all you need is a vision and everything is going to fall into place. But you need all three factors moving in concert for effective change to take place. It is true, however, that *climate* is the place to start. Unless you have a positive climate, neither *logic* nor *vision* are going to grow. Yet once you have established a warm climate in your congregation, you can move to either logic or vision next.

You need to assess whether in fact the climate in your congregation is positive enough, and whether members share a common logic about your mission, to support the final piece, the vision. You might test this theory with your chief decision-making body to see how they view your congregation's climate and logic. If you all agree that your congregation's climate and logic will support a new vision, then it's time to begin!

For Further Reading:

Edwin Friedman. *Generation to Generation: Family Process in Church and Congregation*. New York: The Guilford Press, 1985.
This book will provide lots of "ahas" for pastors, and it is accessible to laity.

Speed Leas and George Parsons. *Understanding Your Congregation as a System: Congregational Systems Inventory*. Bethesda, MD: The Alban Institute, 1993.
This is an especially useful tool in the planning process. We recommend that planning leaders become thoroughly familiar with it and use it with congregational leaders throughout the parish planning procedure. Indispensable to interpreting CSI is another volume, available separately, *Understanding Your Congregation as a System: The Manual.*

Peter Senge. *The Fifth Dimension: The Art and Practice of the Learning Organization*. New York: Doubleday Currency, 1990.
Of special interest to business people in the parish.

Peter Steinke. *How Your Church Family Works: Understanding Congregations as Emotional Systems*. Washington, DC: The Alban Institute, 1993.
Of interest primarily to clergy.

R. Paul Stevens and Phil Collins. *The Equipping Pastor: A Systems Approach to Congregational Leadership*. Washington, DC: The Alban Institute, 1993.
Also primarily of interest to clergy.

CHAPTER 2

Getting Started

Odd as it may seem to you, we, the authors, begin with a reminder that differences of opinion and understanding will naturally arise even in the healthiest settings. In fact, what Rabbi Edwin Friedman refers to as "self differentiation"[1] is a healthy factor in any family system, including a congregation. It is especially important for the leader to maintain his or her individual personhood, ideas, and strength of conviction. So you would be wise to assume there will be rocky moments throughout this process. In fact, any strategic planning process is by its very nature a conflict resolution process. People are going to disagree about where the congregation ought to be going. This organized approach to planning is a way of systematically raising options and allowing people to resolve their differences in healthy, productive ways.

Because differences are to be expected, at a number of points you will find suggestions for dealing with conflict that arises in response to the task at hand. In general, however, the best approach is for leaders to remain calm when disputes arise. If the leaders can convey that they are not shaken by the conflict, the participants from the congregation are unlikely to be shaken. Leaders should also reassure people periodically that the point of this process is to arrive not at unanimity but at consensus about the direction of the congregation.

Here a word of caution is appropriate: If it becomes apparent during this process that there are sharp differences in the congregation over particular issues, it *might* be a signal that at this time the congregation needs to do conflict management work more than strategic planning. (You may need to call The Alban Institute's consulting department and arrange to work with a conflict resolution specialist. When conflict in a congregation is deep and wide, people will simply use the planning process to beat up on each other—and the end result of the planning will not work.) Let us move forward, though, with the assumption that your congregation is a reasonably healthy system without significant unresolved issues.

What Needs to Happen

- Choose a facilitator.
- Select a strategic planning task force.
- Conduct a retreat to help the facilitator, strategic planning task force, and congregational board to get better acquainted, pray together, and prepare for their discernment and planning work.

Why It Should Happen

- The facilitator is needed to spearhead the discernment and planning process.
- The strategic planning task force is chosen to carry out the discernment and planning process because the congregation's board has other responsibilities, and the congregation as a whole is too large to manage the process.
- The task force can also have an energizing effect on the rest of the congregation as each step of the process is undertaken.

How It Might Happen

Choose a Facilitator

The planning process usually proceeds best when a consistent facilitator is present for all sessions. At the very least, someone needs to spearhead the discernment and planning activity within the congregation. While it is often wise to engage the services of a professional consultant, it is not a must. This book is designed so that a qualified layperson can lead the congregation through the entire planning procedure, and you may well have available to you people who already have facilitation skills that will translate to the religious setting. Thus, an early question for the congregation's board to deal with is, Should we engage an outside consultant?

In a smaller congregation (average worship attendance of 100 or fewer), the congregation's clergyperson might well be that facilitator. In larger congregations, it is probably better to have a competent lay leader fill this role. This person will work closely with the pastor to review each step in the process as it arises.

If your board decides to ask a lay leader to serve as facilitator, look for a person with the following gifts:

- Process skills
- The respect of the congregation
- The trust of the pastor
- A grasp of the theoretical material
- Leadership skills
- A rich, consistent prayer life
- A deep sense of commitment to the long-term health of the congregation
- *(Optional)* Some experience in strategic planning in the corporate world, yet an appreciation of the difference between a spiritual discernment process and corporate planning

Although you do not need to engage an outside consultant to facilitate this process, a strong case can be made for engaging a qualified consultant.

- A well-chosen consultant has expertise otherwise not easily obtained in most congregations.
- A consultant brings an outside—more objective—perspective.
- A consultant can be a catalyst.
- People often take an enterprise more seriously when they are paying for professional services in connection with it.
- People ascribe authority to an outside expert.

Another possibility, of course, is a combination effort. For example, an outside consultant might explain the process, lead the earlier congregational gatherings, and then turn the process over to an in-house facilitator.

Whether you choose to engage an outside consultant or to use inside personnel, it is vital that your pastor/priest/rabbi be engaged throughout the entire process. A strategic plan is not going to work without the full cooperation of the head of staff because he or she can effectively bottle-neck any strategic plan. So the head of staff needs to be convinced that this is the best direction for the congregation. Assuming the head of staff is completely supportive of the process does not mean he or she necessarily needs to be present at every single meeting of the strategic planning task force. But she or he needs to give visible support to all congregation-wide meetings. And his or her point of view needs to be listened to and respected as final decisions are made regarding the priorities that are to dominate congregational life over the next four years.

Appoint a Strategic Planning Task Force

After selecting a facilitator to spearhead the discernment and planning process, the next step is to discern the right group of people to serve on a strategic planning task force. It is vital that the pastor and the governing body of the congregation understand the purpose of the strategic planning task force. The group's purpose is not to do the planning and goal setting. Its purpose is in its name: *task*! These are the blessed people who will have the job of continuously processing and distilling the masses of data that will be provided by the congregation as it prayerfully does its work. This task force is not a new power center but a loyal group of committed parishioners who are willing to take on a project that is intense but limited in time and scope.

The task force's responsibility is analogous to making maple syrup. Many gallons of sap are tapped from hundreds of maple trees. This corresponds to the reams of information members of the congregation will provide during the three or four whole-parish events. The syrup maker then takes those gallons of sap and boils them down, just as the strategic planning task force studies and sifts through the information gathered by the congregation. Finally, the sweet and valuable maple syrup is obtained. This corresponds to the final set of goals that will emerge at the end of the discernment and planning process.

Because this task force will help guide the congregation through the entire discernment and planning process, selecting the members of the task force is an important step. It's as significant as the early church's decision to appoint a new apostle to replace Judas as one of the Twelve (Acts 1:15-26) or the decision of the apostles to call deacons to serve the early Christians (Acts 6:1-7). Your governing board would do well to study those Scripture passages to gain a better idea of how the early apostles ended up choosing the people they did.

The optimal size for this task force is five to nine people. Six or seven is best. Fundamentally they must be committed parishioners who understand the process and are willing to work. Ideally, they should represent a cross section of the congregation, with some relative new-comers, some old-timers, people with a variety of theological perspectives, and a balance of genders and any other factors that are significant in your congregation.

Who should pick the task force? The answer depends on the polity and dynamics of this parish. Chances are the governing body will need— and want—to do at least two things:

• Commit the parish to the strategic planning process itself
• Approve the makeup of the strategic planning task force

But the governing body might be involved earlier in the process and asked to help brainstorm possible task force members.

An attractive alternative, if it suits the polity of your congregation, is for the pastor to let the board know that she or he will be working with the facilitator to select possible task force members, subject to the board's approval. This process allows the pastor confidentially to put forward, as necessary, concerns about specific individuals that might be awkward or impossible to bring up at a board meeting. Potential members are interviewed and the process is explained to them. When a list of appropriate, willing candidates is compiled, the task force is then approved by the board.

Once selected, task force members should be prepared carefully so they understand the process and their role in it. The strategic planning task force, a small group dedicated to one task, takes on a role that the entire congregation is too large to accomplish and the governing board is too preoccupied to manage. This group can also continually energize the board and congregation to stay intent on the planning process.

The strategic planning task force operates under a sunset law: When the strategic planning process is finished, the task force is finished. Talented, committed people are often drawn to serve in just such a capacity if they know two things:

- The process involves demanding work, and much will be expected of them.
- The work will be over at a specified time, and they will be able to see the fruit of their labor.

In fact, you should be up front about requirements for participants at all levels. Obviously, much will be expected of the facilitator. The strategic planning task force needs to attend all work sessions consistently and to complete assignments between meetings. The governing board of the parish should be completely informed about and constantly supportive of the process, and should participate in whole-parish sessions.

Members who are not providing specific leadership in some aspect of this process also have an important role to play. Members should especially know that their input at whole-parish sessions is vital. In order to bring members on board and solicit their participation, well before the discernment and planning process begins and as each step is undertaken and completed, they should be well informed about what is happening by means of announcements, newsletters, letters from the pastor, sermons, and so forth. Remember, the whole process may take six to twelve months, and members' enthusiasm needs to be sustained.

Hold an Opening Retreat

The strategic planning task force has been selected and approved by the governing board. Now a joint retreat of the chief decision-making body and the strategic planning task force is held at a time when the most people can attend. It is best to conduct an overnight retreat with shared meals at a comfortable inn or retreat center rather than to hold a long meeting in the church building. Getting away is conducive to creativity.

The purpose of the retreat is threefold:

- To orient participants to the planning process
- To explore several fundamental theories related to healthy congregational life

• To explore goals that might move the congregation to greater health based on the above theories

See that everyone has a copy of the agenda as well as a copy of the "Strength at the Center: A Congregational Health Inventory" (see appendix B) to fill out ahead of time. You might also ask participants to do some reading in preparation for the retreat.

A three-ring binder for each participant will prove increasingly helpful as material accumulates throughout this process. A nice touch is to put a label on each notebook with the individual's name and the name of the group. If there is even the slightest chance that some members will not know everyone in the group, name tags are recommended.

Agenda

1. Gather and move in
2. Eat, relax, and play together (insert meals, free time, and rest into the agenda when appropriate)
3. Pray together
4. Work together
    a. Review objectives of strategic planning process
    b. Review theory on size of congregations
    c. Review the Congregational Health Inventory
    d. Review polarity theory as it relates to effective congregational life
5. Worship together (perhaps celebrate Holy Communion)

Pray Together

Centering

All participants have arrived and moved in. Probably you will have enjoyed dinner together. Now gather in a comfortable room where conversation is easy. The facilitator leads in a centering exercise. The practice of centering is a way of allowing people to let go of all the baggage they brought with them to a session. Centering allows people to focus on themselves for a few minutes Here is a process you can use. (See also appendix C for a more extended, general outline of a centering prayer.)

    I invite you to close your eyes for a moment of quiet reflection. Find a comfortable position. Put your feet flat on the floor with your head, neck, back aligned. Let your hands rest loosely on your lap. From this quiet place, I invite you to become aware of the feelings you bring to this first session. Do you bring feelings of hope—for yourself, for your congregation? *(Pause.)* Do you bring negative feelings about the strategic planning process? Is there something you fear or dread? *(Pause.)* You don't need to do anything about these feelings. Simply note their existence and that they affect your approach to the session.

    I now invite you to focus on your feelings about the people who have decided to join you in this project. How did you feel when you entered the room and saw who was in the group? Which people do you want to get to know better? Which people give you some concern? Know that God can bring healing between you and someone else in this room. Take a moment and say a prayer, asking for that healing. *(Pause.)*

    I invite you now to become aware of your body. Are you holding tension anywhere? Breathe deeply in, out. Each time you exhale, feel yourself letting go of a piece of that tension.

    Now focus on the holy Mysterious One who hovers in our midst, for wherever two or three are gathered together in Jesus' name, there he is in the center. Turn your thoughts to gratitude—for the Spirit active in your life, for all the ways you are blessed by God. *(Pause.)* Allow the Spirit to open your heart to the call to help our congregation.

    When you are ready, when you are breathing easy, long, and deep, when you are relaxed and grounded in grace, slowly open your eyes. Then we'll continue with the session.

Trust Building and Sharing

Give participants the opportunity to risk some self-disclosure. Allow about three minutes for each person to share with the whole group his or her answers to these questions:

- What excites you about taking part in this planning process?
- What concerns you about taking part in this planning process?

Working with Scripture

The following study provides the theological and philosophical framework for the entire process.

Some people advocate what we call a *hierarchical* model for determining a congregation's direction. In this paradigm the great leader hears the voice of God and interprets it for the people, and the people say "amen" and follow. The process followed in this book, however, is collegial, one that has roots in both the Hebrew and Christian Scriptures. God was perceived in community, not hierarchy, at Shiloh, where God spoke to all the people, not just to the leaders. We read the prophecy that the Spirit will be poured out on "all flesh" (Joel 2:28). Paul wrote to the Ephesians, "You are no longer strangers and aliens, but you are citizens with the saints and also members of the household of God" (Ephesians 2:19). And Paul often referred to the Christian community as brothers and sisters "in the Lord" (Philemon 16).

One example of a collegial decision-making method, the first great council of the church, which set a pattern for coming centuries, is recorded for us in Acts 15. A church conflict was presented, debated, and resolved—largely through what appears to be a Spirit-led compromise. To set the stage, some Jerusalem-based believers were going out to Gentile churches and requiring that the men be circumcised to signify that they were followers of the Mosaic Law first and followers of Christ second. A church disturbance ensued, and the problem was brought back to church headquarters. (Have the group members take turns reading from Acts 15:1-29, as they are willing).

Point out the general structure of this account:

Verses 1-5	The core of the argument is laid out
Verses 6-11	The apostle Peter adds an opposing view
Verse 12	Barnabas and Paul describe their experience
Verses 13-21	James, the "senior pastor," offers a compromise
Verses 22-29	A decision is made

Look at two verses in particular:

Verse 22: "Then the apostles and the elders, with the consent of the whole church, decided to choose . . ."

- Who made the decision?
- What is the significance of that for our process?

Verse 28: "For it seemed good to the Holy Spirit and to us . . ."

- Describe the divine and human elements of the decision-making process described in Acts 15.
- What is the significance of that for us as we work together?

Work Together

Review Objectives of the Strategic Planning Process

Let's remind ourselves of the steps still ahead of us.

- Appoint a task group (already done)
- Assess the congregation's ministry
- Reflect on the congregation's history
- Identify the congregation's norms
- Interview key people in the community
- *(Optional)* Survey the congregation to evaluate data already gathered
- Prioritize the goals
- Conduct governing body review and receive approval of the goals
- Share these priorities at a congregational meeting
- Hold a governing board retreat
- Develop a mission statement

Remember that it is not the job of the pastor, governing board, facilitator, or strategic planning task force to set the parish goals. It is their job to facilitate the congregation's discernment of those goals and to distill their input into a final product—to facilitate and distill.

Review Theory on Size of Congregations

Offer an overview of the material below. You might want to examine
only the material on your church's size, but people will probably better
understand the characteristics of your church's size if they have the
opportunity to compare and contrast them with characteristics of other
size churches. Don't forget to consider the significance of a congregation's changing in size as well.

Congregations of different sizes behave in different ways. The most
helpful analysis of this fact has been done by Episcopalian Arlin
Rothauge.[2] He defines four categories of churches: family, pastoral, program, and corporate. The categories are based not on membership rolls
but on average Sunday attendance, not counting Christmas and Easter.
Each category has unique characteristics. The information is especially
important if your congregation is at a juncture point and moving from
one size to another. A congregation pays a price when it changes size,
and a strategy needs to be developed to help make the congregation
aware of that price. If the congregation is looking at growth, a strategy
also needs to be developed to help members decide whether they want to
grow badly enough to pay the price.

1. **The Family Church** (0-50)—Here a handful of leaders function as
matriarchs or patriarchs of the congregation and will have to be on board
with the discernment and planning process. While their power to block is
great, so is their capacity to move change and mission forward. They
give direction and guide important decisions.

In the Family Church, traditions are strong and intimacy is possible.
Decisions can often be made in the parking lot or in other informal settings, rather than in formal meetings. The pastor fills a roll akin to chap-
lain. On the down side, leaders are also gatekeepers, and it may be hard
for outsiders to break in.

2. **The Pastoral Church** (50-150)—Here congregational life centers
around the ordained leader. Within a leadership circle of people closest
to the pastor, small groups represent different interests, such as the board,
the patriarchs and matriarchs, and newcomers. Farther from but still centered around the pastor are a fellowship circle and a membership circle.

In this size congregation, the opinion of the ordained leader is paramount. She or he must endorse the planning process if it is to move ahead. A small strategic planning task force can be a powerful force for change. On the down side, Pastoral Churches have an incredible unconscious resistance to growing into program-size congregations. If a congregation's average worship attendance is between 110 to 130 or more per Sunday, you can expect subtle resistance to growing any further. Members fear that the intimacy this congregation holds as one of its special characteristics will be lost. In addition, members are concerned that as the congregation grows, the intimacy members enjoy with their pastor and the pastor's availability will be lost because she or he will be busy taking care of all those "new" people.

Any congregation of this size that seeks to engage in a strategic planning process should reproduce the article on congregational size found in appendix D, circulate it for discussion, and then deal with the issue at a specially called congregational meeting where the chief question to be resolved is, Do we want to grow into a program-size congregation? The answer that comes forward may be quick and positive, yet the cost of growing larger needs to be taken seriously by all members. They will need to grieve the loss of what they were in order to become a Program Church.

3. **The Program Church** (150-350)—The chief operating mode of this congregation is no longer relational but organizational. When leaders and members consciously organize to build relationships and to foster effective, faithful ministry, the result is a program. The ordained leader becomes enabler and chief administrator. Elected leaders become responsible for programs. A number of the program units surround the pastor. The pastor needs to coordinate the efforts of each program unit and see to it that the programs have capable leaders, and that the spiritual and relational needs of those leaders are being met.

Ministry in this size congregation can become task oriented, and relationships can suffer. On the other hand, small group programs and other systems can be successfully developed to facilitate communication and familiarity among members. Developing lay leadership becomes a central task for the ordained leaders.

For the purposes of strategic planning, it is vital that pastor, board, and carefully chosen strategic planning task force members coordinate their expectations and activities. Ongoing communication with members is more difficult than in smaller churches, so tools like a newsletter take on added importance. This size congregation is already used to mobilizing itself into small groups, which will be helpful at several planning stages when members are asked to perform specific tasks in small groups.

4. The Corporate Church (350 and up)—It is the multiple staff that most clearly distinguishes the Corporate Church from the Program Church. The ordained staff members function as specialized resources for program areas. The pastor becomes the head pastor and can even take on legendary qualities. Surrounding the staff are circles of governing boards, primary leaders, secondary leaders, and subdivisions of group life.

Members may have difficulty gaining access to the pastor and may need to make an appointment. Those who wish to have a close relationship with the pastor are unlikely to get it. They are more likely to find their primary connection to the congregation through other staff specialists or lay leaders.

Congregations of this size and organizational style have the ability to offer specialized programs, a significant benefit. While Family or Pastoral Churches probably could not offer a ministry for, say, divorced singles in their forties, a Corporate Church could and would probably do it well.

Naturally, strategic planning in a Corporate Church is more complex, and communication tools like newsletters take on added importance. As we noted above in the example of Ladue Chapel, the staff resources available to a congregation of this size and budget permit a style of process management not possible in a smaller church but necessary in the large church. Ladue Chapel was even able to engage the services of a temporary data technician to continually collate and distill the mass of data gathered at each activity, then to feed the information to the strategic planning task force, pastor, staff, and board.

5. Congregations that are changing in size—One of the most devastating or invigorating things that happens in any size congregation is movement from one size to another. Some congregations are growing rapidly. Others are shrinking. The important thing to remember is that all change is difficult. Quite possibly the most difficult change is the move from being a Pastoral Church to being a Program Church. Everyone is stretched, and people have the clear impression that the once "available" pastor is now harder to reach. The logic of numbers, of course, explains this change, but feelings aren't logical. We recommend to you Arlin Rothauge's work, *Reshaping a Congregation for a New Future.* He correctly notes, "Whether the size increases or decreases, the health of a congregation shows in how well it reshapes for a new future."[3]

If your congregation is in transition between sizes of congregations, two things increase:

- the need for strategic planning to manage the changes occurring
- the need to be aware during the planning process of the heavy role change is playing in your congregation's life

A more complex and complete description of the four sizes of congregations, with an emphasis on the special leadership requirements of each size, is provided in appendix D, "How to Minister Effectively in Family, Pastoral, Program, and Corporate Sized Churches," a report by Roy M. Oswald.

After presenting information about characteristics of churches of different sizes, ask retreat participants to discuss the following questions:

- Which of the above four models describes us best?
- How does the description fit? How does it not fit?
- Are we changing in size? How does that affect our life together?
- What are some implications of our size for (1) how we organize ourselves to do strategic planning? (2) what we need to plan for?

Review the Congregational Health Inventory

Before the retreat, participants should have received and filled out "Strength at the Center: A Congregational Health Inventory" (see appendix B). The purpose of the inventory is to help congregational decision makers to assess the congregation's health based on key elements needed for congregational growth and vitality. The goal is to develop a strategic plan that has the potential of moving the congregation toward greater health, which in turn will lead to various kinds of growth. Instructions for evaluating participants' responses are included in the appendix.

Review Polarity Theory

Polarity theory states that tension is actually a good thing in a congregation. *Polarity management* provides a useful tool for diagramming congregational tensions. In turn, this visual aid helps us make sense of the
tension in a congregation and begin to envision ways to manage tensions
to the group's advantage.[4]

A key principle of polarity theory states: Problems can be solved;
conflicts can be resolved; but polarities can only be managed. Polarities
are unsolvable and unavoidable. Your only choice is whether you will
manage them well or manage them poorly.

Self-Esteem/Humility

Take the polarity "self-esteem/humility." These two human qualities
each have both a positive side and a negative side. The positive side of
self-esteem is having the capacity to honor or value yourself. Yet when
we overemphasize self-esteem, we get caught in the negative side—
grandiosity. When we think too highly of ourselves, we need to move to
the positive side of humility, which gives us an immense sense of freedom from self-concern. The truly humble person does not continually
need to draw attention to himself or herself. But we can also get caught
in an overemphasis on humility, which get us into self-deprecation, the
negative side of humility.

What makes this a polarity is that the negative side of each pole is
corrected by moving to the positive side of the opposite pole. In this way,
the poles are interdependent, and there is no way out of the dilemma. In
truth, there is no human being who does not struggle with this polarity.
Rare is the individual who is so perfectly balanced between these two
poles that at all times and in all circumstances he or she can maintain that
balance. In fact, it is usually when we find ourselves on the negative side
of one of these poles that we realize we need to move to the positive side
of the opposite pole.

This is how the self-esteem/humility polarity looks on a map.

+	+
Honoring yourself Valuing who and what you are Having a healthy self-regard Having confidence and a sense of self-worth **Self-esteem**	Freedom from self-concern Having no need to draw attention to yourself Not thinking more highly of yourself than you ought to think **Humility**
Grandiosity "I'm better than anyone" -	Self-deprecation "I'm worse than anyone" -

Everyone one of us regularly deals with many more personal polarities. Where, for example, do you usually end up on this polarity?

+	+
Look before you leap.	**He who hesitates is lost.**
-	-

Law/Grace

Look at a theological polarity as another way of learning how polarities work. "Law-grace" is a polarity. Both are gifts of God, yet they are interdependent gifts. The one is meaningless without the other. This is the way it would look on a polarity map.

+	**+**
Convicts of sin Makes God's demands clear Points the way to redemption **Law**	Offers us forgiveness Sets us free Restores us to wholeness **Grace**
The demands are too great Under God's judgment, we are reduced to rubble Those who think they obey all God's laws become self-righteous **-**	"Let us eat, drink, and be merry, that grace may abound" Without the demands of the law, grace is meaningless Grace feels soft and mushy, it can be cheap grace **-**

If you think you understand how polarities work, let us consider several that are more central to developing a strategic plan for congregations.

What does it mean to be a disciple?

Most of us would agree that a primary task for each congregation is to make members into disciples. A transformation needs to take place as we move more deeply into dimensions of grace and faith. People need to be transformed *from* being centered on themselves and what the congregation can do for them, *into* servants who ask what they can do to serve God, given their gifts and talents.

Is personal transformation a painless process or a traumatic one? Is becoming a disciple an easy process or a difficult one? If the answer to the two questions is "both," then we are more than likely involved in a polarity that needs to be managed—an unsolvable, unavoidable issue that every congregation must face. You will know whether your congregation is managing it well or poorly by observing how much time you spend in one or both of the negative quadrants of the polarity map.

+   **+**

Few or no demands are made of newcomers.

Because we do not ask much of people, no one is frightened away.

We emphasize grace.

We make it as easy as possible to become one of "us."

Easy	**Difficult**

Discipleship

Newcomers are challenged to turn to Scripture and prayer for guidance.

A year-long catechumenate is offered to all who want to become members.

"Easy come, easy go."

Membership means little.

We are losing members out the back door as fast as we are bringing them in the front door.

"If this is all it means to be a member, then why bother?"

Some people are scared away.

Some get self-righteous because they have gone through such a demanding process.

Expectations are too difficult for some.

Clergy don't know how to make disciples out of members.

-   **-**

Work Polarities with a Group

To begin working on a polarity in a group, draw a polarity map on the floor using wide masking tape. The map should look something like this:

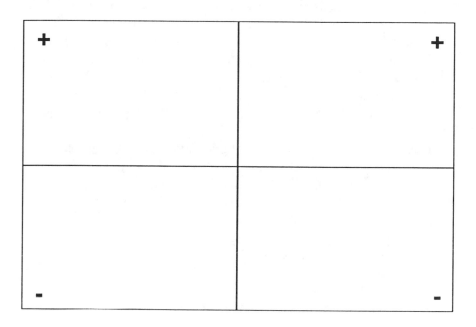

Copy the discipleship polarity above onto a sheet of newsprint, or project it on a screen using an overhead projector. Then have group members divide into four groups, each with at least two but no more than six members. Each group should stand in a circle in a quadrant of the floor map. At least one person in each group needs to have a pen and pad of paper to take notes.

Make sure group members know which quadrant of the discipleship polarity they are standing in. Then ask them to brainstorm for three minutes all the things they can think of that apply to that quadrant, while the note taker jots down their ideas. Group members should expand considerably on the original map. At the end of three minutes, call time. Ask each note taker to tear off the sheet of paper and to place it face down in the quadrant where he or she has been standing. Then ask all the groups to move clockwise into a new quadrant. Repeat this process until all four groups have brainstormed in each quadrant for three minutes..

Ask each group to stay in the quadrant where it has ended up and to pick up the three sheets of paper already in that quadrant. Give each group a sheet of newsprint, and allow them fifteen minutes to collate the four lists into a single list describing life in that particular quadrant.

Ask each group to tape their sheets of newsprint on a wall, placing them according to the original map—the two positive sheets on the top, and the two "easy" sheets on the bottom. Gather the whole group around the expanded polarity map, and ask one person to read the list in the positive/easy quadrant. Then ask someone to read the negative/easy list, followed by the positive/difficult list, and finally the negative/difficult list.

This process will help the group to grasp more fully the complexity of the polarity. Ask retreat participants to discuss the following questions. (If your group is large, ask members to form groups of no more than six and to discuss the questions in their small groups and then to report their ideas to the whole group.)

• Does this polarity apply to us? If so, how are we managing it—well or poorly?
• If we are managing it poorly, what one or two goals might we propose to address the issue in our strategic plan?

Quite possibly this is the only polarity you will have time to consider seriously on your retreat. Polarities strike so close to the heart of congregational life that you might need to limit yourself to dealing with only one core polarity. Much depends, however, on how deeply the group engages this first polarity. If group members have gotten involved in a heated discussion about the way your congregation goes about helping members become disciples, you might want to stop right here. Your congregation might not be able to plan for any more than revising your strategy of disciple development. If, on the other hand, this polarity does not really grab anyone as a particularly serious issue for your congregation, you might want to proceed to the next polarity, "movement/enterprise."

What is the church?

Movements generally do not last long. Perhaps you have been part of Cursillo, Marriage Encounter, or a human relations laboratory. These can be powerful and transforming experiences, but even though follow-up experiences and gatherings are provided, often the experience fades. It is only when we institutionalize the experience that it has a chance of surviving.

Yet we are all too aware of the downside of institutions. They usually end up being self-serving, because at an unconscious level, all institutions seek first to preserve themselves. But the determination to survive leads a group far from the original movement they had hoped to preserve in the first place. Some congregations have followed this path, straying far from the movement from which we were born.

Here is a polarity—an unsolvable, unavoidable dilemma for congregations.

+   **+**

Emphasis on conversion and a
changed life

High energy, high commitment

Passion, enthusiasm, joy

Freedom, spontaneity

Flexibility to respond quickly
to needs (not hindered by
tradition, "That's they way we've
always done it.")

Strong connection between
faith and life

Strong sense of community

Resources freed up for mission,
not maintenance

Evangelical, seeking new
members

Revival, renewal, redirection of
of institutions

Confrontation of and challenges
to institutions

Raises up leaders

Hopeful, promises positive
vision of future

Providing permanence, foundation, nurture for leaders, center
and focus, shape for movement,
cohesion, continuity, visibility

Linking faith and culture

Building on dependability, sense
of place and identity

Support of wider outreach, global
possibility, connectedness with
other institutions

Sense of ownership about greater
resources, shared leadership

Movement   **Enterprise**

Lack of center, focus   "We've always done it this way"

(continued)

(continued)

Freedom for heresy, negative message	Loss of vision
	Rigidity
Individualism, chaos	Professionalization of leaders
No quality control, no identity	Resistance to change
Lack of loyalty, commitment, discipline	Idolatry of institution
	Tendency toward exclusiveness
No plum line or continuity	Coldness, calculating style
All heart, no head	Lack of power to transform
Self-righteousness	Focus on power
Leader-centeredness, danger of charismatic leader	Loss of vitality caused by effort to maintain institution
Exclusivity, closed sytem	Leader burnout
Burnout	Institutions unconsciously seek first to survive; their very life often subverts the mesage they are to represent
▬	▬

The movement begins in the movement/positive quadrant. A congregation in this quadrant refers often to the Scriptures and feels a direct link with the founder. Many Christians would like to believe that they, and their church, can stay here indefinitely. But inevitably the negative side develops, and in the movement/negative quadrant, we find moribundity, discouragement, misinterpretation. At this juncture, the group moves diagonally upward to institution/positive. Here continuity of the faith is ensured, Scriptures are preserved, and leaders (especially clerical leaders) get increasingly professional training. This is good. It serves the purpose well. But eventually the group moves to institution/negative. Faith becomes weak, and the institution becomes self-serving. The

natural move is (diagonally upward) "back to basics," to the "pure teachings." Keep in mind, this a polarity and cannot be frozen at some imagined ideal point, and it is vital for the health of the congregation to manage the movement.

The polarity has to do with ways congregations renew themselves
spiritually. Remind your congregation that institutional survival and
health will always tend to take precedence over re-grounding ourselves
in the basics of our religious movement. Every church institution needs
to hold a spiritual "revival" of some sort every few years. If it doesn't,
institutional needs will dominate. After explaining this polarity, ask re-
treatants to respond to the question, Where are we in this picture?

Again, if group members really get into the notion that your congregation is not managing this polarity in a healthy way, you might need to
spend your time developing some goals about how your congregation
will manage this polarity. This might be enough for this strategic plan.
If so, do not consider the remaining polarities presented here.

The next polarity, "journey out/journey in," asks how well your
congregation is managing the flow between feeding members spiritually
and then sending them out for the difficult task of being the church in the
everyday world.

How do we live out our faith?

+	**+**
More mission opportunities	Grounding ourselves once again in the Spirit
Visiting the Sick	
Witnessing	Building relationship with God and others through spiritual food, refreshment from prayer, and Bible study
Getting out of yourself (good for depression)	
Relieving pastor of workload	Strong relationship with God that carries over into everyday life
Accepting responsibility for helping others	Openness to external things that touch our lives
Strong foundation	
Outreach in all the community	Mysticism
Visibility of the church	Becoming excited again about God's word for us
Good News	
Ecumenical attitude	
Sharing talents with others	
Journey Out	**Journey In**
Burn out, over extension	Overemphasis on feeding "me" only
Resentment that others seem to be doing little or nothing	Judgmental attitudes
Neglect of our own parish family	Lowered standards
Losing sight of God	Excessive navel gazing

(continued)

(continued)

Discouragement, joylessness	"It's not my job," Let someone else do it"
Feeling exploited	Illusion that we have done enough
Forgetting *why* we need to serve others	Self-centeredness; we can engage in spiritual narcissism, forgetting that faith needs to be active in love
−	−

Whole congregations can move along this polarity, as can individuals or groups within congregations. In the journey out/positive quadrant, we find the activists, people who are oriented toward action and doing. Their faith is alive and prophetic, and because of them change happens. But the down side is that people are not fed and soon are out of resources for their work. The logical move (diagonally upward) is to the journey in/ positive quadrant. Here we find the contemplative spiritual style. The soul is nourished and grounded. The downside to this is everything that goes with religious individualism. So we move again diagonally upward to prophetic action.

Keep in mind this a polarity and cannot be frozen at some imagined ideal point, and it is vital for the health of the congregation to manage the movement. Again after explaining this polarity, ask group members to discuss the question, Where are we individually and corporately in this picture?

Next Steps

Before retreat participants begin to leave, take care of the following tasks:

- If you have not already done so, establish a planning calendar. Include regular task force meetings, congregational events, task force and governing board joint meetings, and other steps in the discernment and planning process.
- Remind strategic planning task force members that this is not a committee that goes on forever! They have signed on for a process that will take six to twelve months, and then it will be over.

Closing

Remind participants that you are engaged in a spiritual discernment process and that therefore you need continually to ask for the guidance of the Holy Spirit. This means that every gathering will end with prayer. Find your own format for this prayer. If the pastor is present, you may want to end with a celebration of Holy Communion, especially at the end of a long gathering such as a retreat. Or someone in the group may lead participants in a devotion designed for this event. Group members may like to form a circle, hold hands, and invite everyone to offer a simple petition. Or you may simply want to stand for a time of silent prayer, concluding with a brief prayer of blessing. Find out what feels most comfortable to everyone, recognizing that prayer is not always a comfortable thing.

CHAPTER 3

Ministry Assessment

Before jumping at a vision for the future, your congregation needs to see clearly its strengths and potential liabilities. The work of Kennon Callahan in his book *Twelve Steps to an Effective Church* is especially helpful here. Callahan is quite emphatic about the need for a congregation to identify its strengths and to build on and expand a few strengths selected by the congregation. The planning process should not be seen merely as an opportunity to fix what is broken. We need to feel good about ourselves as we look into the future, rather than to wallow in our failures and shortcomings.

The planning polarity illustrating this should shed some light on why it is important to begin with strengths.

+	**+**
Pride	Vision
Past/Present	**Future**
Problems	Anxiety
Complaints	
-	**-**

In this polarity, we move first from problems and complaints to pride, then down to engage our anxieties about the future, and finally up to an exciting new vision for our congregation. In order for us to deal with our initial anxiety about a vision for the future, we need to move to the positive quadrant of past/present. This is pride. When we can reflect on our past with pride, affirming how we have trusted God to get us through rough spots, then we can build on these strengths for the future. We are then much more able to deal with the down side of the future which is anxiety. When people are sure the essential goodness of the parish is not going to be sacrificed for some grand vision, they are then much more able to enter the process with lowered anxiety.

In this segment you will be offered three options for doing a ministry assessment.

- Reflect on your congregation through the lens of Scripture, using the pattern found in the Book of Revelation of addressing letters to churches.
- Investigate the early marks of the church—*kerygma, didache, koinonia, and diakonia.*
- Provide four incomplete statements as discussion starters.

We recommend that the assessment activity you choose take place in a member's home and that every member of the congregation be invited to participate in this activity. We have found that breaking up the congregation into smaller groups is manageable in all sizes of congregations—family, pastoral, program, corporate, where the Sunday attendance is seventy and where it is twelve hundred or more. The discernment and planning process works just as well whether thirty-five home meetings must be arranged or only two are necessary. Furthermore, it is rare to find a congregation of any size in which anywhere near 100 percent of the active members will come out for such events. While heavier participation is always more desirable, a representative cross section is just as valuable for gathering the data we are after.

What Should Happen

- Consolidate, record, and interpret data gathered from as many small group evaluation sessions as possible.
- Create a composite evaluation of your ministry together.
- Establish top parish priorities (interim, not final).

Why It Should Happen

- To set goals intelligently, you need an accurate appraisal of where you are now.
- The best evaluator of where you are now is the congregation itself. Thus, you are looking for as broad a participation as you can achieve.
- Discussion in small groups is likely to be more open than discussion in groups with more than twelve members.

How It Might Be Done

- Prepare your strategic planning task force to plan and lead home meetings. (Each task force member should lead no more than three

home meetings. Recruit additional trainers as needed to keep the work load manageable.)
- Hold the home meetings and gather the data.
- Meet with the strategic planning task force to collate and distill the data.

Pray Together

Begin your training meeting with a simple centering exercise, such as the one here. (Or refer to appendix C for another example of centering prayer.)

Centering

Let's go inside and be quiet with ourselves. What things do you notice when you take the opportunity to focus completely on yourself? What primary sensations are you receiving from your body? (*Pause.*) What feelings seem to dominate your life at the moment? (*Pause.*) Let's also be grounded in our sexuality. How are you feeling about yourself as a woman or a man right now? (*Pause.*)

Let's also become aware of another reality present with us. Right now God is raining down upon us an abundance of grace, God's unconditional positive regard for us. Here in this room there is more grace than any of us can use. Let's relax into it. When we are open to it, this grace relaxes and heals every place it touches. Breathe in this grace and allow it to go directly to any spot that seems to need the healing power. If you are hurting emotionally, allow this grace to penetrate your soul and to transform that part of your life. (*Pause.*)

Now imagine yourself going back in time to visit the church of your childhood. If you remember several churches, pick the one that had the greatest impact on you. Envision yourself as a child seated in a pew in that church on a Sunday morning. See if you can look around and esti-mate how many people are with you in that church. (*Pause.*) What images return to you as you revisit that church?

(*Pause.*) Besides Sunday worship, recall some favorite memories of your life with the people in that congregation. (*Pause.*)

Return to an awareness of your breathing. Check once again to see that your body is relaxed. When you are ready, slowly open your eyes. We will then continue with the rest of this session.

An alternative approach to centering is to use a centering prayer approach (apophatic prayer) and ask people to work in silence on three basic segments:

- Ask God what God considers the strengths and liabilities of the congregation.
- Allow space for God to respond.
- Summarize your sense of God's message to you in a word or phrase and begin repeating that word or phrase in time with your breathing.

Participants can then either share their experience with everyone (if the group is small) or in pairs (if the group is large).

Trust Building and Sharing

- Limit this section to fifteen minutes.
- Ask group members to take one minute to describe any anxiety they may be experiencing as they contemplate leading a meeting in someone's home.
- Ask, What is your best-case scenario of what could happen in such a home meeting? What is your worst-case scenario of what could happen at such a meeting?

Working with Scripture

- Provide task force members with Bibles, prayer books, hymnals, or another source, and ask them to read responsively or in unison Psalm 27:1-14.
- In Psalm 27 the psalmist talks about great fear. Ask group members to talk about the encouragement we can derive from this passage.

Work Together

Introducing the Home Meeting

Small group theory has shown that a group with any more than twelve people will begin to allow some group members to hide in the corner and not participate. A "home meeting" is a gathering of not more than twelve people, generally held in someone's home, that allows people a greater sense of freedom to talk and share openly. Just as most people will not see the church or temple worship space as a place for expressing opinions aloud, most people do regard a casual home setting as a place to do just that.

It is not necessary that members of the strategic planning task force hold these home meetings in their own homes. In fact, meetings can be held in a comfortable spot in the church. And it would be better to have other members of the parish act as hosts for the meetings, with a member of the strategic planning task force chairing the discussion portion of the meeting. When the hosts are chosen well, you will have a good cross section of the congregation serving as hosts.

In order to ensure the broadest participation of members in these home meetings, have the hosts call specific members of the congregation to invite them to attend a meeting. Try to arrange the guest lists so members are invited to homes where they will feel comfortable expressing their points of view. Thus, for example, certain groups will be made up entirely of baby boomers, while other groups will include mainly retired people, and so on. As you collate the data from these meetings, you will then have some idea of how certain segments of the congregation feel about their congregation.

In addition to the host and the member of the strategic planning task force who will chair the meeting, you can also invite members of your chief decision-making body to take part in the meetings. This will help governing board members get in touch with the way various groups think about things in the congregation.

We suggest taking some time here to go over with participants the Acts 15 model for corporate discernment. You may well want to make use of the material in "Working with Scripture" in chapter 2. This focuses us on why we are doing what we are doing and why we are doing it this way,

Objectives for Home Meetings

- Create a warm, accepting environment where people are willing to share their joys, pain, hopes, and concerns about your parish.
- Engender a deeper bond between individual members—and between members and the parish.
- Elicit the wisdom and concern of committed members that will inform a dynamic strategic planning process.
- Retrieve this data in forms that can easily be integrated into a strategic plan.

Proposed Design for Home Meetings

- Gather informally and enjoy simple refreshments.
- Open with a prayer.
- Introduce facilitator and host. Briefly introduce the task force and explain the importance of this gathering.
- Conduct a team-building exercise. Be sure to explain that confidentiality will be maintained. Their comments will be reported accurately, but names will not be attached to the comments. Then encourage each person to share briefly:

  - name
  - how long he or she has been a member
  - what originally attracted him or her to this congregation

(An appointed recorder will be taking notes. If necessary, the facilitator can take notes instead. This team-building activity in itself provides important data.)

Remind the participants that their input is valuable, and that we are engaged in an assessment of the ministry of the whole parish—not just the lay leadership or the pastoral leadership. The parish includes all of us! (Negative responses are welcome and valuable, but try to keep the tenor of your meeting positive.)

Assessing Your Ministry

We have provided three ways to lead members in reflecting on their perceptions of the strengths and liabilities of your congregation. You will need to decide which method suits your congregation best, or which method the members of your strategic planning task force feel most comfortable leading. You will probably want to use the same format for all the home meetings so you can more easily compare data, although you might use these gatherings in another way to garner the data you need to make plans for your congregation. Prepare strategic planning task force members to lead home meetings using the method you have selected by actually following that procedure as a group.

Bible Study on Revelation

Lead a Bible study on Revelation, focusing on the "angel" of the congregation. Have everyone open their Bibles to the book of Revelation, and have participants read the first three chapters. You might go around the room and ask each person to read a verse until you have completed the three chapters. Or you might ask for volunteers to trade off reading portions. Then allow forty-five minutes for open discussion of the chapters. Ask open-ended questions such as the following to spark conversation:

- Look at Revelation 1:10. What could John be referring to when he talks about being "in the Spirit on the Lord's day"?
- When John speaks to the "angel" of a church, what could he be referring to?
- What seems to be the general intent of the letters to these seven churches?
- Is there any discernable pattern to the letters?

Revelation was written during a time when the early church was under persecution. It makes use of magnificent poetic imagery, and we need much visual imagination to grasp its meaning. After some discussion of the passage to help participants understand the notion of the "angel" of your congregation, give each participant paper and pencil and allow thirty minutes of silence while they go get something to drink and then go off in a corner to think about the angel of your congregation. They should try to use the basic format of the seven letters they just read.

After half an hour, have participants reconvene in groups of three or four and read their letters to each other. (If your whole group has eight or fewer members, ask each participant to read his or her letter aloud to the whole group.) Allow time for discussion after each letter is read. This sharing and discussion activity should take half an hour, and then call the whole group together.

Hang two sheets of newsprint on the wall, and ask one person to be recorder for each sheet. One piece should have the heading, "For this, I commend you." On the other, write, "But this I have against you." Take half an hour to write down participants' responses for each list.

Explain to participants that this activity has helped identify strengths of the congregation on which you want to build in the next few years, as well as point of weakness or lack of faithfulness you want to correct. The strategic planning task force will use these lists to prepare interim goals that will be considered at the end of the process by the whole congregation for implementation. Ask whether group members would consider turning in their letters at the end of the evening to the strategic planning task force member chairing the meeting. Letters do not need to be signed. Close the meeting with prayer.

Kerygma, Didache, Koinonia, Diakonia — How are we doing?

A discussion might also be organized around the marks of a true Christian congregation as defined by the church leaders back in the first and second century of the church. The early church leaders were concerned about how they could tell whether some congregation way out in Asia Minor was really the true church of Jesus Christ. After much discussion, the church fathers decided that a number of factors would have to be present before the congregation could really be considered a true church of Christ. These marks of the church are as follows:

- *Kerygma* (proclamation)—Is a message of faith, hope, and love being preached on a regular basis in that church?
- *Didache* (a sub-category of kerygma)—Is the quality of the instruction given to children and the converted worthy of the Gospel?

- *Koinonia* (fellowship)—Do members of the community care for one another and newcomers in a way that truly represents the compassion of Christ?
- *Diakonia* (service)—Is this church reaching out beyond itself in some way to serve the poor, the destitute, the outcast, and the like?

In many ways these are still excellent categories with which to evaluate the health of a congregation. Ask group members to respond to the questions in the first four segments of the Congregational Health Inventory, which are organized around these four categories. Members may complete the questionnaire at the home meetings, although you might prefer to send the questionnaires out ahead of time so people are already prepared to discuss the questions once the meeting gets under way. (You might also ask a cross section of the congregation to complete the inventory, in addition to the group completing the inventory for the home meetings. Then incorporate the cross section's responses into the data gathered at the home meetings to prepare interim goals.)

Lead the discussion by simply walking through the questionnaire and inviting people to share their responses to the questions. Try to make sure everyone has a chance to share their perceptions and no one is allowed to dominate the discussion. At the end of the meeting, ask participants to turn in their questionnaires to the strategic planning task force member present. The task force member who gathers the questionnaires could then collate the data and summarize it for the rest of the task force. Or the discussion could be recorded in some other way so that data can be reported back to the whole task force.

Fill in the Blanks

You might want to simplify your meeting by using four questions to help participants communicate their feelings about the congregation. These questions could be handed to people as they enter the home or could be mailed out ahead of time.

The four questions we recommend are:

1. If our congregation did not continue to _____, I would lose interest in remaining a member.

2. The things that concern me most about our congregation are
   _____.
3. If our congregation would _____, I know I would call my friends
   and telling them what wonderful things they are missing.
4. If with a stroke of a pen I could change one thing at our congrega
   tion, I would _____.

Next Steps

Facilitators should let people know how the gathered data will be used
and when home meeting participants will have additional opportunities
to give input and hear about results and final plans.

    Congregation members should be specifically invited to participate
in two upcoming events, one to reflect on the congregation's history and
another to reflect on the congregation's norms. (Refer to appendix E for
an explanation of norms.) People at these home meetings who have
questions or concerns should also be invited to contact either members
of the strategic planning task force or board members, who will be creating the final strategic plan.

Closing

Close your home meeting with a prayer. (You might form a circle and
pray the "Our Father.")

Summarizing the Home Meeting

Regardless of which method was used for the home meeting, following
each home meeting, *on the same evening as the meeting,* the member of
the strategic planning task force chairing the meeting should review the
recorder's notes about the meeting and complete the following statements as a way of pulling together his or her immediate thoughts about
the meeting.

1. Three key insights I have coming out of this meeting are _____.
2. As people look into the future of this congregation, they focus their anxiety on _____.
3. As people look into the future of this congregation, they expressed optimism about _____.
4. My sense is that _____ keeps these people invested in this congregation.
5. The task force needs to direct attention to the following areas of concern:
6. People want to plug in to these places:

Facilitators should also select a time when they can do a simple collation of any written forms used during the meeting, plus notes taken on comments made. Facilitators should be prepared to report on this collation at the next strategic planning task force meeting.

Other Training Issues

If members of your strategic planning task force remain anxious about taking a leadership role in these home meetings, take some time at this or another gathering to role play such a meeting. Have one member of the strategic planning task force lead the rest of the group in the discussion method you have chosen. Allow group members to raise questions and concerns about the discussion method and their responsibilities. As issues arise in the group discussion, talk through what alternatives a facilitator might have in such a situation. Remember, too, that the input from the strategic planning task force is just as valuable as that from each home meeting, so record the responses from your role-played discussion and save them for collation later.

Remind home meeting facilitators that no matter which discussion method you use, all meetings should be kept within the announced time period. Most people want to know when they make a commitment what to expect and how much time it is going to take.

Ending the Training Session

Before ending your training session, the following matters should be addressed:

- Is there anything task force members need to conduct their home meetings?
- Exactly when and where will home meetings be held? If someone other than task force members will be hosting the meetings, scheduling obviously needs to be coordinated with the hosts. Try to schedule meetings for different times of the week to increase access for the congregation.
- Set or confirm the next task force meeting date.
- Pray, simply and briefly, for each other and for your congregants, with expectancy and faith that God is up to something good here!

Promotion

Recruit someone to work with the pastor (and quite possibly the parish secretary) to publicize the upcoming home meetings. Use every means available. Post sign-up sheets at church. Ask the pastor to make announcements about the events. Write letters for the parish newsletter and ask members to call the church office to sign up for a meeting.

An invitation from the pastor to all members can be helpful. The letter should cover the following points:

- This is an opportunity to provide vital input that will affect the direction of the parish for the next several years.
- The congregation's leaders and this process are grounded in prayer. Together members are seeking God's plan for the parish.
- The process follows a biblical model for seeking corporate direction.
- This assessment is not of our leadership but of the ministry of the whole parish.
- Those who attend home meetings will be asked to talk about what they like about the parish and what concerns they have about it. (If you like, describe the core of the selected discussion methods.)

Collating and Distilling the Data

After the home meetings have been held, strategic planning task force members and any others who facilitated or served as recorder for meetings gather to collate and distill the data gathered. Use the following process.

Pray Together

Open the meeting with prayer. You might use a centering prayer based on the model provided in appendix C. Or use this process:

1. Ask people to relax, as for centering prayer, and then to sit with the question, "God what are you trying to say to us through the people who have participated in these home meetings?"
2. Let everyone sit in silence and pay attention to any answers that come to them.
3. Ask everyone to think of a way to summarize their sense of God's message, and then to repeat that word or phrase silently in time with their breath.
4. Ask everyone to share their responses with the whole group or in pairs, depending on the size of your group.

Trust Building and Sharing

Ask each person to take one minute to respond to two questions:

• What for you was the high point of your home meeting?
• What was the low point?

After members share, acknowledge that the strategic planning task force is a lot of work. Ask task force members how the experience is stacking up against their expectations. Remind them that a "sunset law" applies to this committee! In just a couple months the labor will be finished and they can hand off their work to others.

Working with Scripture

Ask several group members to read portions of Matthew 20:1-16. Then invite discussion of the parable:

* There's an old adage that in volunteer organizations: "Ten percent of the people do ninety percent of the work." What is your response to that?
* What is Jesus saying to us in this parable?

Work Together

Data Collation and Distillation

Regardless of which method you used for gathering information at the home meetings, home meeting facilitators and recorders should take turns reporting as specifically as possible on responses to the process questions. A recorder should record responses, noting which items are repeated and how often. Combine similar concerns, still keeping track of how often an issue was mentioned. Look for major themes that seem to evolve from all the data. Also note any obvious issues that seem to be missing. Use these steps for gathering the meeting responses.

Step 1. Ask each member to read their responses to the questions they responded to following the home meetings. Once all the responses have been read ask, "What appear to be the key issues raised at these meetings?" Ask someone to record these key issues as they are identified.

Step 2. Revelation Bible Study: If you used the Bible study on Revelation, you will want to hear what people wrote in their letters to the "angel" of your congregation. If you have fewer than twenty letters, you could ask group members to read the letters. If you have more than twenty letters, ask group members to collate and summarize the main points of the letters from the groups they facilitated. Once again ask, "What appear to be the key issues raised at these meetings?" Add issues to the list already in process.

Congregational Health Inventory or fill-in-the-blanks questionnaires:

Each member of the task force should come to the collation meeting with a summary of the written inventories or questionnaires. Ask each person to use these summaries to report to the group on their findings. Again, add to the list in process from step 1.

Step 3. Ask the task force to review the key issues that have been identified at the home meetings and to decide how each issue should be dealt with. Much of the material will not lend itself to implementation through a long range strategic plan. Some information might be referred to church staff, to the governing board, or to specific committees. But some of the issues can be translated into interim goal statements.

Setting Goals

The evening needs to end with the task force putting on newsprint six to eight key goals to address the most important issues raised in the home meetings. Prepare one or two goals for each of these four growth areas:

- *strengths* to build on
- *dysfunction* in our congregational life that needs to be fixed
- *mission* to our communities
- *aspirations* for the next four years.

The goals are to be filed for later, when your task force and your chief decision making body will enter a discernment process to choose which of twenty to thirty are central to the future health and vitality of the congregation. Recognize that the work you are doing at this meeting is simply one step along the way toward that final discernment time.

Goal setting is not easy work. Each goal should have the following characteristics:

S - Specific
A - Attainable
M - Measurable

Specific: Avoid global goals, such as, "We strive to become a more loving community." The more specific the goal, the more helpful it will be. Try: "We will strive to have every member of our congregation warmly greeted on Sunday morning by at least six people, at least two of whom they have never met."

Attainable: If the goal is not attainable for your congregation, given its members and resources, it will only serve to discourage members. Each goal needs to have some stretch to it and engage the congregation in some hard work, but it still also needs to be within reach.

Measurable: At the end of a period of time, you should be able to measure whether or not the goals have been completed. In fact, you ought to be able to measure the progress of a goal as it is unfolding. This is important so the congregation knows when it can celebrate the accomplishment of any goal.

A further note on setting goals. You need to distinguish between goals, objectives, and action plans. A goal is the overarching end product that you want to include in your congregation's life. Objectives might be thought of as sub-goals; they contribute to completion of the goal. Your action plan is the specific strategy you intend to implement to make sure each objective is reached. Here is an example:

Goal: To raise morale in our congregation, prevent lay leader burnout, and facilitate greater bonding among members by conducting more fulfilling and productive meetings.

Objectives:
1. To ensure that every meeting in this congregation begins with at least fifteen minutes of team building and ends with at least fifteen minutes for critique.
2. To prepare and send out in advance to all participants a written agenda for every meeting in the congregation.
3. To conduct training session for all those chairing meetings to equip them to run more efficient meetings.

Actions Plans:
1. In January, to call together all current chairs of committees and have them brainstorm ways to improve the quality of meetings in the congregation.

2. In February, to conduct a training seminar on running effective meetings.
3. In May, to survey committee members to find out whether meetings are becoming more effective.
4. In June, and so forth.

It is not necessary that objectives and action plans be completed for all interim goals developed this evening. If objectives occur to people, you may record them, but the objectives need not be extensive or complete. Action plans are usually designed after a goal has been chosen as a high priority by the congregation.

Make sure a summary of the major findings from these home meetings gets into the hands of the pastor, church board, and strategic planning task force members. Communicate the findings to the congregation as a whole, too. Work with the person responsible for the newsletter to see that at least a summary gets in the next issue. You might also find bulletin board space in the church where information can be posted and add more material as the process develops.

Remember that we are working for a broad sense of participation in the whole planning process. Make it clear that this is just the beginning and in no sense a final product.

Next Steps

Remind strategic planning task force members that the next step in the process is a gathering to reflect on the congregation's history. This is a whole-parish event. This step has always proved to be enjoyable. People relish getting in touch with their past. Inevitably people, including some of the old-timers, will say, "I didn't know that about us." The newcomers will be fascinated with the spiritual journey of the congregation they have joined.

Closing

Ask group members to name something for which they are thankful.

CHAPTER 4

An Evening of Historical Reflection

As we look back on the sands of time, we probably see God's footprints alongside ours. It is important that we perceive and acknowledge that God has been with us. We also need to notice that our forebears were able to place their trust in God and then to continue their own journeys. Being aware of God's past presence with us and our forebears gives us confidence that God will continue with us into the future.

In one sense, our sacred Scriptures are simply an accounting of how God interacted with God's people through a period of time. In a similar vein, each congregation has its own sacred history and needs to refer from time to time to its own "scriptures"—the history of a congregation as it is passed along from one generation to the next. Your prayers prior to this event should be that you will discern the presence of God within your congregational family throughout its history.

What Should Happen

- To your growing data bank of information about your congregation, add goal statements that spring specifically from the congregation's history.
- Involve congregants in the excitement of the ancient art of story-telling. Collectively piece together *your story*.
- Gratify and enlighten old-timers and newcomers alike as you record the experiences of the years.
- Process the information you gather:

- Turn the story into statements of meaning about your congregation.
- Prioritize these in order of their relative importance in your organization's life.
- Turn these data into interim goal statements.

Why It Should Happen

- It is impossible to understand the present without understanding the past.
- Mapping the behavior of key players in the family's or congregation's past sheds light on family or congregation behaviors of the present.
- Every congregation has myths about itself, as well as a history composed of positive and negative experiences.
- It is only when we come to terms with the past that we can move freely into the future.

Facing the Past

The axiom, "Those who do not learn from the mistakes of the past are doomed to repeat them," holds true of the congregational family. As any pastor who made the mistake of ignoring what happened under his or her predecessors ruefully admits, the past will rise up and overtake the best laid plans for the present anyway. Thus, in this chapter we provide a systematic and attractive way to coax the skeletons, along with the pleasant memories, out of the closet and into the daylight where we can examine them.

Loren Mead cites "coming to terms with history" as one of the developmental tasks of a congregation. It is only when a congregation is able to look at itself squarely and say "For better of worse, this is who we are" that it can also say "Now, what do we want to do about this?"

Every congregation is powerfully shaped by its history. We know every congregation has a unique personality, and each has a unique "angel." The way the congregation began way back some 30 or 130

years ago already began to shape its personality. Was the congregation
a break-off from another congregation? Was it founded because of the
special vision of one person? What do we know about that person and his
or her dreams?

Between its beginning and the present, any congregation has had
many ups and down, good times and not-so-good times. Likely at an
unconscious level, many members long for the days when the congregation was feeling up and everything was clicking on all cylinders. As the
congregation has called each new pastor, it likely has been hoping this
pastor would lead them back to days of glory. As we reflect on the reality
of these pastorates, it is important to ask, When that pastor was not able
to take us back to glory days, how did we cope? Were we able to learn to
experience the grace of God even in down times?

When working with nuclear families, systems therapists will often
use a genogram or similar device to map the generational background of
each of the key players in the nuclear family. The past sheds an astonish-
ing amount of light on the behaviors (functional and dysfunctional) of
the present family. To help a congregation look at its family story, we
want systematically and lovingly to coax the skeletons, along with the
pleasant memories, out of the closet, so we can examine them in the
light. If only we could truly unpack that story and know ourselves from
the inside out. Perhaps that would allow us to take our own destiny in our
hands and to shape an alternate culture that builds on our strengths and
no longer supports the self-defeating patterns of the past.

The Power of Myths

Every congregation has at least one myth about itself. (When we use the
word *myth*, we don't mean it as it is often misunderstood—as something
untrue, unreal, or not factual. A myth is an explanation of why things are
the way they are. A myth can thus in some ways be more true than a set
of facts derived from the five senses.) We all know how powerful myths
are. Myths shape the way we perceive reality, and they tend to perpetuate
themselves because people consistently live into the myths they believe
about themselves.

When a congregation's myth is too divorced from reality, there can
be real pathology in that congregation. For example, when the myth is

that we are a warm, caring, friendly congregation, yet behind the scenes people are butchering each other with gossip and mean-spirited actions, there is no way the congregation can grow in a healthy way. This type of congregation may attract new members, but more than likely these new members have on some level sensed that games are being played in this congregation, and they have unconsciously decided they could gain something by getting involved in the back stabbing. This is where new-comers can help perpetuate pathological behavior.

In contrast, healthy congregations have healthy myths about them-selves. The split between the myth and reality is not great. Newcomers can sense that the congregation it really trying to live up to what members say about it. Generally the myths have developed from something that happened in the congregation's past that really helped the congrega-tion grow spiritually. Healthy congregations need to engage in historical reflection so they can really celebrate the great things that have happened in their past, a past worth celebrating because the members now are reap-ing the benefits of those positive myths.

Every congregation has a history made up of both positive and nega-tive experiences. It is only that some have had more positive experiences than negative, and others have had more negative experiences than posi-tive. In either case, consciously going back into those histories and trying to bring to consciousness the myths we believe about ourselves will most likely have a positive effect on a congregation. Congregations that have really experienced and reflected on their self-destructive times have likely grown deeper spiritually because of them. Underneath it all we should be asking, "What can we learn from this?" This then is where we shift from sociological analysis to spiritual discernment. We now lift up our history and seek to discern the hand of God leading us.

Peter Senge in his popular book, *The Fifth Discipline: Developing Learning Organizations*, says about vision:

> Vision is a set of guiding principles and practices and shared pictures of the future that provide energy that draws us into the future. It is not a leader's charisma, not a crisis for which people galvanize into action, not a cookbook with step by step instructions. Vision is the picture that we carry around in our heads of what we want to create, a sense of commonality that binds people together for the greater good, and that uplifts people's aspirations. Vision binds people together around a common identity and sense of destiny.[1]

Senge's understanding of vision is similar to what we mean by myth: both reflect a community's self-understanding, and both draw a community into the future. This view of vision casts a whole new perspective on what a congregation needs to do in order to discern what God is calling it to be and do. Senge seems to suggest that a vision already lies buried somewhere in the unconscious parts of a congregation's life. In order to develop a new strategic plan, the task of the strategic planning task force is to assist a congregation to uncover the vision that is already there and to test whether this is, in fact, the vision we desire to support.

Based on the myths a congregation believes about itself, its vision might be to minister faithfully in ways that demonstrate the love of God and effectively meet the needs of the poor, the lonely, and the outcast in that community. Members of such a congregation have much to celebrate and certainly new members will be attracted by its vision. On the other hand, a congregation's vision might amount to a faded, self-effacing shrug: "We will never ever amount to much, so why would anyone ever want to become part of us?" It is only when this vision is unearthed that members will be able to say, "Let's change this." Regardless of a congregation's myths about itself, it would be foolhardy even to attempt a strategic plan without first coming to terms with history. Only if the plan addresses that history can we ever move toward greater health.

How It Might Be Done

"A Night to Remember" is a method workable in many situations. Participants in this evening will:

- have fun remembering
- record the parish's history, as they recall it
- develop "meaning statements" growing out of those remembrances
- prioritize the meaning statements
- begin to develop goals based on the meaning statements

This exercise has been done with groups as small as fifteen and as large as 150 and we have found that the people involved have fun, and more important, that an incredible amount of energy gets released in this activity. You will want to do some careful preparation for this event and work with the folks in the parish who are most skilled at planning events. The people managing this planning and discernment process might decide they want to begin the evening with a potluck supper or other special event. If you begin with supper at 5:00 P.M., you should plan to begin work on the history at 5:45 and to finish about 9:00.

It is vital to obtain an outside facilitator to take you through this process. Neither the pastor nor lay leaders of the congregation should facilitate this part of the design, even if they have the facilitation skills to pull it off, because they are members of the parish and have an investment in the history of the place. When someone makes a comment about the congregation that this person does not agree with, she or he might have a hard time putting it on the newsprint. Better to have someone who knows nothing about your congregation and is not invested in the history being expressed a certain way. If you have not engaged an outside consultant, a neighboring clergyperson with good facilitation skills might be invited to come in and lead your group through this exercise.

Hold the meeting in a large room but not in the worship space. Post on a wall up to twenty feet of newsprint. On the far left of that newsprint write "Congregation's Beginning." Even though parish histories are not determined by the clergy, nevertheless most congregations recall their history by pastorates or rabbis. Print each pastor's or rabbi's name and the years of his or her tenure from left to right along the top of the newsprint. (Be careful to get accurate data.) Along the bottom of the newsprint, note secular historical events to remind people of the history of common life.

This format makes it easier for people to connect congregational events with events in the rest of the world. A congregation might notice, for example, that its fortunes have waxed and waned with the nation's prosperity or lack thereof—that things were "up" during Ike and "down" during the Vietnam War. Or people might notice that the congregation felt the pain of a local mine or factory closing long after the actual shutdown.

Recording Your History

Let participants know that you will be leading them in a centering prayer at the end of your time together. For now, simply offer a prayer asking for group members to have wisdom, humility, and a spirit of charity during your work.

As much as possible, gather the entire group around the newsprint on which you are working. Ask participants to call out the most important events that took place during each pastorate, beginning with the current pastorate and working backwards one pastor at a time. You will want to write quickly but neatly, budgeting your time well. With a large group, ask one or two people to assist in recording the information as it comes. The facilitator simly repeats the words that are to be recorded. Some discussion of the events is helpful, because it can shed light on the *emotion* surrounding that event. On the other hand, too much discussion may bog down the flow of the evening. When you have reached the end of a particular pastorate, move to the next back in time. Eventually, you will get to a point where no one living remembers. Then begin to record stories that have been handed down. Keep this part of the process flowing and try to finish it in under an hour and a half. At the end of your remembering, you will have a valuable twenty feet of history on the wall. You may well want to leave it up for one or two weeks, particularly inviting old-timers to add to it and newcomers to view it.

People will want to know whether to put scandals in print on the wall. This is a valid concern. On the one hand, it would be historically invalid and unhelpful to pretend nothing happened. On the other hand, we do want to be careful not to smear character or hurt the feelings of those with different perceptions. The facilitator must be sensitive. Be tactful, but do not ignore alarming bits of data. Record them with a qualifier like "rumors of . . ." or "disagreement about . . ." If serious argument developes, the facilitator should say "Let's acknowledge that we have some serious difficulties here, and then move on."

The most important reason for doing this remembering exercise is to record the congregation's perception of what happened. This is fascinating to old-timers and newcomers alike. Old-timers enjoy their special role in this evening. Newcomers find the history of their adoptive family a matter of considerable interest. In fact, event planners might want specifically to invite old-timers and newcomers to this evening. Newcomers have an especially important role in the next segment. They will likely be more objective in their analysis of the history than some of the old-timers.

Developing Meaning Statements

What does our history mean? The next step is to develop "meaning statements" or generalizations based on observations about this history. It is best to do this right away, while the information is fresh in everyone's mind and right in front of them on newsprint. Patterns will inevitably emerge, and at the end of the evening you will select the most important of these. But begin simply by generating a list of these generalizations or meaning statements.

Pass out a list of sample meaning statements. You might have participants take turns reading them. These do not describe your church, of course, but they give you an idea of what meaning statements are.

- Food seems important to us around here. We love our potluck dinners.
- Whenever we engage in a building program, we seem to get a new spurt of energy.
- There never seems to have been a time when we were not fussing over something. It almost seems as if we get our energy from our little internal squabbles.
- This congregation has never had a big stewardship effort. Maybe our consistent lack of money is tied to this?
- We have always shied away from conflict. It feels as if conflict-avoidance behavior is a main source of difficulty.
- It appears that the women have carried this congregation for the last twelve years. Also, we have had no specific activity for men in the last ten years. What has happened to our men and men's programming?

Divide into small groups, preferably with no more than six per group. Each group should spend thirty minutes writing down meaning statements for your parish based on analysis of the historical data you compiled. Each group will need a facilitator to keep it focused. If the proportions are right, a member of the strategic planning task force could fill that role well. She or he may be the spokesperson for the group later.

Prioritizing the Meaning Statements

Return to the large group. A spokesperson from each group reports the group's list, while the facilitator (or scribe) writes brief notes on each observation, creating a master list of observations. As groups report, consolidate statements that repeat an observation. As a large group, work together to choose the most important positive and negative generalizations about the congregation. Keep the process moving along and focused. This should take less than thirty minutes.

Important negative statements identify issues the congregation must confront if it is to become healthier and increase its opportunities for growth of any kind. Important positive statements point out qualities so central to the life of the parish that you would be foolish to abandon them. The goal is to isolate qualities that need to continue—or change— if this system is to have a viable future.

Voting

Number each meaning statement. Each person in the room has three votes to identify what he or she thinks are the three most important meaning statements—positive or negative. Give participants several minutes to decide which three statements they think are most important. You can tally the votes in any of three ways.

- Go around the room and ask each person to identify his or her choices by number ("I vote for numbers 2, 6, and 14") and then put checks next to those statements.
- Go down through the list and have people raise their hands to indicate their votes and write the total for each item on the newsprint.
- Give each person three sticky dots and have them place their dots next to the statements they think are most important, being careful not to cover up another dot. (In a large group, this is probably the most efficient way of handling the process. Call a coffee break and have people take turns placing their dots on the sheets during the break.)

Be sure to broadcast the results of this activity as widely as possible.

The idea is to reinforce the importance of the work done by the congregants present. It also helps those just watching the planning and discernment process to come on board. One congregation came up with these:

1. When the Gospel is preached, the parish grows in every way, moved by the Holy Spirit.
2. Throughout most of the congregation's history, there has been a loving fellowship that keeps people in the congregation.
3. We need more clearly defined areas of responsibility filled by more people.
4. Outreach is important. In times when outreach was stopped, parish finances fell; when outreach was part of the focus, finances in creased.
5. There always seem to be strong factions in the parish family. Some times differences have been handled peacefully, sometimes angrily and stormily. When power centers (rector, vestry, parishioners) have been in conflict, enrollment has diminished. When power has been in balance, the parish has flourished.[2]

Closing

Lead the group in the following centering prayer.

Before we go our own ways this evening, let's be quiet for a moment and reflect on our time together. If you have something in your lap, put it on the floor. Get your chest, neck, and head in a straight line, and put your feet flat on the floor. Close your eyes.

As you think back on this evening's activity, what feelings were strongest? Did you have feelings of gratitude and pride for your congregation? When did you feel that way? *(Pause.)* Was there any time when you felt anger about what took place sometime in your congregation's past? *(Pause.)* How about fear? Did you at any time this evening feel afraid as you looked into your congregation's future? *(Pause.)* Even these negative emotions can be seen as positive. They could be translated into a sense of concern for your congregation.

Now think about the things you would miss most about this congregation if it, by some imaginary catastrophe, disappeared from the face of the earth. What would be the most difficult losses for you to deal with? *(Pause.)*

Take some time now to imagine this congregation twenty years in the future. See if you can visualize this congregation as a strong, viable community of faith supported and nourished by your children and grandchildren and those of your friends, plus a whole bunch of new people who have moved into this area. You might be in the picture, too, many years older than you are now. What things of lasting value for you do you hope will still be a strong feature of this congregation far down the line? What elements of your congregation that surfaced tonight do you hope will continue long into the congregation's future? *(Pause.)*

For our closing devotional this evening, I would like you to do two things. First, pair up with one other person and share some of the things that occurred to you in this reflection. Choose a partner with whom you have not had much contact lately. Try to select someone other than your spouse. Maybe choose someone you do not know at all. Allow this brief prayer time to be a way to get to know that person a little better. Go ahead and choose a partner now.

Focus your sharing on what you would miss most about this congregation if it were to disappear. In addition, what qualities do you hope this congregation will still consider central to its life some twenty years down the line? You will each have three minutes to share. *(Pause for six minutes.)*

Now I would like the two of you to move into prayer. You might not be used to praying with just one other person. If that is the case, let this be your first experience. Allow times of silence. Feel free to express gratitude for all that your congregation means to you. Feel free also to express your hopes and concerns as you look into your congregation's future. After a few minutes, we will all close by saying the Lord's Prayer together.

Developing Interim Goal Statements

Strategic planning task force members should meet as soon as possible after the evening of historical reflection to turn the top priorities into goal statements. One or two goals should be written for each of these growth areas:

- *strengths* to build on
- *dysfunction* in our congregational life that needs to be fixed
- *mission* to our communities
- *aspirations* for the next four years.

If the meaning statement is a positive one, the goals statement should focus on how the parish might capitalize on that strength. For example, "Music has always been a strength of this parish; we propose getting this message out to the community in the following ways . . ."

If the meaning statement is negative, goals should focus on ways the parish can move beyond that damaging dimension. For example: Our congregation's indirect way of dealing with conflict encourages gossip and drains our energy for ministry. To counter this we will:

- conduct a six-Sunday adult forum on healthy ways of dealing with conflict;
- develop ground rules to follow when someone hears gossip or negative comments about another member, such as encouraging them to deal directly with the aggrieving person;
- ask the pastor to preach about the positive side of conflict, including (1) how we might use conflict as a way of building positive energy in the parish; (2) how various biblical characters dealt with conflict in constructive ways.

Whoever does this work should note that these are interim goals to be added to the list already accumulating, and that the final list of goals will be narrowed down at the end of the strategic planning process.

Next Steps

- Confirm the date for the next congregational activity, "An Evening of Norm Identification." Your job that evening will be to assist a small group in identifying norms.
- Between now and then, encourage all strategic planning task force and governing board members to read the handout, "Norms: Every Church Has Them" (appendix E).
- Confirm the next strategic planning task force meeting date.

CHAPTER 5

An Evening of
Norm Identification

Confession and Absolution

Over time, congregations develop patterns and ways of doing things. Often after a time, the congregation no longer examines these patterns. When we worship, we take time for self-examination and confession, and we do much the same thing in this planning process.

Every congregation has both implicit and explicit expressions of its corporate life. Often a congregation through creeds and mission statements asserts what it believes or would like to believe about itself. This is its explicit expression of its beliefs and values. No congregation can totally live up to its explicit statements about itself. If it could, grace would be unnecessary. Yet it is important that a congregation ascribe to beliefs and values that are a constant challenge to it. Every congregation needs to aspire to become more than it already is. One aspect of that aspiring is identifying and confronting its self-destructive patterns. Otherwise, it just becomes a group of people who sit in comfortable pews, and religion becomes simply a way of sanctioning members' present lifestyles.

A congregation begins to disintegrate when it allows its way of living and acting to depart radically from its beliefs and values, when it stops trying to walk its talk. When this happens in an individual, a psychological professional would say the person has dissociated (has departed from reality or is suffering from schizophrenia). Such dissociation is just as unhealthy in an organization as in an individual.

Visitors and newcomers notice quickly when a congregation lacks integrity and authenticity. Rather than being attractive to these visitors or newcomers, the community actually becomes ugly. Hence, the need for the kind of self-examination we are describing here. Does the way we live our life together reflect what we claim about ourselves?

There are a variety of ways to assess ourselves. Several ideas may have occurred to you already. You might find it effective to ask a congregation to spend an entire evening identifying its norms—unwritten rules by which it lives. Through this process, what goes on at an unconscious level is raised to consciousness and is examined. What is "under the table" is put "on top of the table" where we can examine it, talk about it, and even change it.

Prepare people for the fact that this may not be pleasant. Some of the process is not supposed to feel good. Yet we rely on our experience with confession and absolution (pardon, forgiveness) to carry us through this activity. If the evening does not have a certain "bite" to it, the group is probably either confused about the task or avoiding or denying something.

What Should Happen

- Identify your "norms"—those unwritten rules by which you live— in order to grasp fully what is dysfunctional and needs to be fixed.
- In an all-parish setting, identify six to twelve different norms and then rank them in order of importance to you as a group.
- Finally, have the strategic planning task force rewrite them as necessary, so they will be useful when you establish your top priorities.

Why It Should Happen

- We are committed to a systems understanding of the congregational family.
- If the congregation is going to identify its top priorities, then it is going to need to have a high degree of corporate self-understanding.
- Norm identification is a way of assisting the group to bring to the conscious level, where it can deal with them, values that are normally in the corporate unconscious.

This is probably the hardest concept in the planning and discernment process for the group to grasp. However, careful attention to the homework and use of concrete examples will produce understanding and eventually real fruit. A spiritual discernment process always engages first the truth of who we are as a community. We read in Scripture, "If you continue in my word, you are truly my disciples; and you will know the truth, and the truth will make you free" (John 8:32). Most of the time we really do not believe that. We avoid facing the truth about ourselves and as a result remain slaves to our misconceptions about ourselves. In short, this step in the spiritual discernment process prepares a group of faithful people to say to God, "All right God, we now see ourselves truly for the first time. Now what do you want us to do about this?"

This evening of norm identification provides you with another opportunity to view your congregation as a system whose parts are inextricably tied to each other. What ties people together are the unconscious agreements that "we will all behave in a certain way." People who violate these unconscious ways of doing things will be punished in one way or another, even when the rules have never been stated. ("People are just supposed to know these things. There is something wrong with them if they don't.")

This step in the process provides an opportunity to review these norms and to differentiate between the positive ones and the negative ones. In our strategic planning process we will then accentuate the positive norms and develop strategies to counter the negative ones. Some specific examples may shed some light on this. Suppose, for example, a norm in your church effectively says the only people who can decide who gets to use the good china that has been purchased for the church are a handful of wealthy matrons. Sooner or later someone is going to violate that norm and there will "be hell to pay." We can only hope the violator is not a new member who came from another congregation where everyone was welcome to use whatever dishes were available in the church kitchen. The blow-up may cause this newcomer to leave the congregation, never to return. As a matter of fact, when you seriously look into your history, you may find you have lost several families over the issue of the church china.

An example of a positive norm could be that whenever something is not right, people speak their minds. People enter into disagreement frequently in this congregation. They have learned how to fight hard but fairly, and how not to take the disagreement personally. In this congregation, rather than dealing with disagreements through gossip and back stabbing, they go directly to the person with whom they have a disagreement and share their concern openly. This congregation has had the good fortune of having a specific person in its history who modeled this behavior for others and who seemed to have a great influence on the congregation.

How It Might Be Done

Make sure the strategic planning task force and governing board read and understand the handout, "Norms: Every Church Has Them" (appendix E). If possible, get the handout into the hands of every member of the congregation. You might want to insert it in Sunday bulletins, incorporate it in the regular newsletter, and so forth.

Pick an evening when as many members as possible will be able to attend, and set aside about two and a half hours for the actual work. You might plan to begin with an ice cream social at 6:00 P.M., and then allow 6:30 to 9:00 for norm identification.

When participants have gathered for the evening, make it clear to them that everyone should expect to work hard during the evening and that you will honor the agreed-upon schedule. Then outline the agenda for the evening:

- Open with centering prayer
- Review the concept of norms
- Talk generally about customs participants have noticed in the congregation
- Engage in a small group activity to help members discover the congregation's norms. Report these in plenary session.
- Identify which norms the strategic planning task force needs to address

After any other housekeeping matters have been tended to, turn to prayer.

Pray Together

Centering

I invite you to close your eyes, relax your body. Breathe deeply, exhaling the tensions of the day. Peel off your work and home concerns as if they were a bulky coat you don't need indoors. Focus on the unbelievable grace of God. *(Pause.)* There is no question that right now, at this very moment, there is more love being poured down on you than you can possible absorb. We are in relationship with a God who is ever more ready to bestow love on us than we are ready to receive. God's love for you is sure. It is a question now of your ability to love yourself. Just for a moment, see if you can see yourself through the eyes of God. Look at yourself with total, unconditional, positive regard. Continue for a moment to bask in this unconditional love. *(Pause.)*

Now shift your focus to this congregation. Reflect on what makes this place different from any you have known before. Imagine yourself sailing a half mile above this place. The roof is off and you can look down on the congregation. Observe the congregation at worship. Observe them during weekday activities. Do you notice how people's behavior changes, just subtly, the moment they set foot inside the building? *(Pause.)* Every human system is run by unwritten rules that govern behavior within that system. What positive and life-enhancing rules do the people in this parish live by? *(Pause.)* What negative and life-diminishing rules do they follow? *(Pause.)*

Finally, picture yourself walking into church. How does your behavior change when you set foot inside the door? How is your behavior different from the way you act at work? at home? How is your dress different? your language?

Now focus again on your breathing. When you sense that your body is relaxed, slowly open your eyes.

Trust Building and Sharing

As a way of getting the group immediately engaged in thinking about norms, have them form groups of two or three. Ask each person to take one minute to complete this sentence:

The one custom of this parish that I have never quite gotten used to is . . .

Working with Scripture

Read Matthew 13:45-46, and then invite participants to reflect on the verses. You might ask them, as they move through the evening, to keep in the back of their minds this question: What do we really value around here?

Work Together

Norms: Every Church Has Them

Using appendix E, explain to the group what norms are and how they work. Then explain that they are going to be identifying your congregation's norms—the unwritten rules you live by—so that the norms can become even more grist for the mill that will be producing your top priorities as a congregation. Let participants know it is important that they enter into tonight's exercise thoughtfully and prayerfully. What they will each contribute is key to your collective future.

On a sheet of newsprint, draw a big circle and write the word *norms* in large letters. Then around the circle write the categories of all the norms you hope to explore during the evening. You might also want to invite participants to contribute other possible categories they would prefer to explore. Consider the following categories: children, men/women, conflict, money, treatment of clergy, newcomers, use of the building, who is welcome here, and expectations of "real" members.

Ideally, you want one small group of three to ten people working on each category, so depending on the size of the group, you might want to limit how many categories you explore. Do not worry, however, if you need to ask groups to take more than one category, or if several groups work on the same category. Once a set of categories has been agreed on by those gathered, either assign people to work on particular categories, or let participants choose which one or two categories they would like to work on.

Ask each small group to take a sheet of newsprint and to record their hunches about the norms of your parish for the assigned category. Small group members should try to choose norms they think will yield the most important information you need to know about yourselves and how you behave with one another.

The first reaction of most participants is, "We don't have any unwritten rules about children" or "We welcome everyone here." Another great temptation will be to begin talking about the ways things "ought" to be. Neither approach is what we are after here, though. This is about the way things are. What are the real (though probably unspoken) rules we have for this particular category? Encourage participants to put their aside skepticism and to identify their sense of any norms. Invite them to give their intuition free reign. Groups that do this move from uncertainty to a sense of wonder about their discoveries: "This *is* what we live by here, isn't it?!"

If small groups are working on more than one category, make sure someone calls time to keep the groups moving at the right pace to cover both categories. When the groups are finished, call everyone back together. Ask each group to tape its newsprint to the wall and to report on its conclusions in each category it tackled. At the end of each report, invite the rest of the participants to offer feedback. Do you think the group accurately identified your congregation's norms? Do you see norms to add to the list? Cross off the lists items that do not receive the support of most of the large group. Consolidate where needed.

Using the voting process described in chapter 4, ask participants to indicate which norms are most important to the life of your congregation. One congregation identified the following norms as key:

1. We have a low key approach to newcomers because we don't want to be seen as pressuring them.
2. We tend not to follow through with decisions, especially those that affect kids.
3. We tend to shy away from major conflicts. We try to keep them molehills rather than mountains. As a result we tend to stifle any type of strong exchange between members.
4. Money intended for outreach tends to be directed toward material crises, not toward evangelism per se.
5. We accept the presence of men without asking for more than their presence.[1]

Closing

Offer this prayer for guidance:

> Heavenly Father, in you we live and move and have our being. We
> humbly pray you so to guide and govern us by your Holy Spirit that
> in all the cares and occupations of our life we may not forget you,
> but may remember that we are ever walking in your sight. Amen.
> *(Adapted from* The Book of Common Prayer *according to the use of
> the Episcopal Church [New York: Oxford University Press, 1992],
> p. 100.)*

The Strategic Planning Task Force

As before, meet with the strategic planning task force to review the evening of norm identification, to evaluate its meaning, and to prepare for
the next step. Take some time to review and collate the data gathered at
the evening of norm identification. Go over the norms developed at the
congregational event. Is this an accurate reflection of your congregation?
Does it square with your own understanding? Does it square with your
work to date?

As you did following the home meetings and the evening of historical reflection, identify the most pressing needs for change as you move
toward greater health as a congregation. Begin identifying interim goals
that will address these changes. Once again one or two interim goals
should be prepared for each of the following growth areas:

- *strengths* to build on
- *dysfunction* in our congregational life that needs to be fixed
- *mission* to our communities
- *aspirations* for the next four years

The above-mentioned church's strategic planning task force took the
top-rated norms and turned them into these interim goal statements:

1. It is important to welcome newcomers without high-pressuring them.

2. We need to exercise follow-through (for example, with children's programs and other projects). We need to continue and finish what we start.
3. When conflict arises, we need to be up-front with problems.
4. We need to begin to direct some outreach funds toward evangelism.
5. We are consciously going to recruit the men of this congregation to become specifically engaged in congregation activities.

This might be a good time to ask yourselves how well you are keeping members involved in this task of developing a strategic plan for the congregation. At the end of the process, remember, you first and foremost want the congregation to own the results, the top priorities. Therefore, they must feel that their input has been heard along the way. Even those who "only stand and watch" must have a sense that they have been part of the process. Are you making use of these forums to disseminate the results of our work to date?

- the bulletin board
- the newsletter
- the pastor or rabbi (through sermons, announcements, letters)
- your own discussions with other members

Next Steps

- Confirm the next strategic planning task force meeting.
- The next step involves interviewing key people in your community to get an accurate picture of the mission field immediately around your congregation. The next chapter begins with a meeting of the strategic planning task force to prepare to conduct the interviews. Depending on how long the norm identification follow-up process takes, you might elect to begin preparing for the interviews at the same meeting.
- Close the task force meeting with prayer.

CHAPTER 6

Interviewing Key People in the Community

In this step, we ask the question, What is God calling us to be and do in this community? Our biblical witness attests that we usually find God in the places of deepest pain. Do you discern God already at work in the places of pain and suffering in your community? Is God calling you as a congregation to address one or two of those painful situations? Which issues suit your resources, your faith stance, the concern of your people? As the environment and the issues surrounding a congregation change and as the congregation itself changes, differing responses to these questions will emerge over time.

When we review the life of Christ, we continually see him addressing the pain of the poor, the outcast, the alienated—doing the sacrificial thing. As we affirm our allegiance to Jesus' way of worshiping God, his path of compassion, what jumps out at you? Where would Christ be if he were simply wandering around your community today?

What Should Happen

- Ensure that outreach to your community is part of the congregation's thinking as it formulates its primary goals.
- Interview the people best qualified to assess our community's needs, the people most directly involved in its life.
- Ask these civic leaders two questions:
  - What do you think are the most important needs in our community?
  - How do you think a congregation our size could help meet those needs?

Your congregation's expression of interest in meeting at least some of
the community's perceived needs will improve the surrounding community's perception of you.

Why It Should Happen

- Experience has shown that congregations tend to focus on their internal, maintenance needs first, and a church focused in on its own
  survival will generally decline.
- A telling aphorism often heard in parishes is, "Charity begins at
  home." This generally means, "Let's take care of us before we look
  to the needs of others." "Home" is more than the place where we
  worship. It includes the community around us.
- Even if most of your church's members no longer live near the
  church, members who assume responsibility for the church's neighborhood find that their involvement helps them personally.
- This exercise is intended to help a congregation develop a vision and
  action plan for ministry in and to the community.

How It Might Be Done

- Introduce the strategic planning task force to this three-step process:
  - Gather to plan
  - Conduct the interviews
  - Gather to collate the interview findings

Open the planning meeting with prayer.

Pray Together

Working with Scripture

Remind the task force that it is vital for the group to keep connected to
God's purpose in the work we do. We learn much from Scripture about

listening to God. Ask several people to read aloud 1 Kings 19:1-15. Then ask group members how they hear God. Few of us hear God's still, small voice, but when people do, generally they do not hear it with their ears but within themselves. Let's experiment with a type of prayer that opens us to hear God this way.

Centering

We're going to spend a few moments in contemplative prayer. The early church practiced two basic forms of prayer: kataphatic prayer and apophatic prayer. In Western Christianity we are generally taught the kataphatic form of prayer, which is active and filled with words, images, and concepts: "Dear God, thank you for the sunshine this morning. Be with Aunt Doris as she struggles with cancer."

The apophatic form is the prayer of the mystics, who felt we cannot contain God in words or images. Their aim was to empty themselves to make room for God. To experience God, they moved toward silence rather than words. They spoke of "waiting on God." To quiet the mind for this type of prayer, the mystics repeated certain sacred words or phrases to keep their minds from wandering, to keep them in quiet awareness of the wonder of the present and God's presence. Different formulas have been used over the years. A phrase central to Judaism is the "Shema," Deuteronomy 6:4 (NIV): "Hear, O Israel: The Lord our God, the Lord is one."

For centuries Christians have said the "Kyrie," from the Greek "Kyrie eleison," which means simply, "Lord, have mercy." Likewise, Christians have offered the "Jesus prayer" under their breath: *(while inhaling)* "Lord Jesus Christ, Son of the living God," *(while exhaling)* "have mercy on me, a sinner." Another simple sacred phrase is *(inhaling)* "I am"; *(exhaling)* "thou art." The point of the words it to help the one praying to focus on his or her own being and God's being. Another prayer is the "Ave Maria": *(inhaling)* "Hail Mary, full of grace, the Lord is with you." *(exhaling)* "Blessed are you among women and blessed is the fruit of your womb, Jesus. *(inhaling)* Holy Mary, Mother of God, *(exhaling)* pray for us sinners now and at the hour of our death. Amen."

Christians who have prayed in this manner have sometimes

said they feel as if they are placing their hearts into the heart of God. They have learned to pray all day long by repeating such a phrase, even while engaged in manual labor. Perhaps this is what St. Paul was referring to when he said, "Pray without ceasing" (1 Thessalonians 5:17).

Let's stop our busy minds for five minutes and try this form of contemplative prayer. Close your eyes. Relax. Choose a prayer to offer, and repeat it in time with your breathing. Whenever your mind begins to wander, gently call yourself back to the simple phrase, reminding yourself that you are in the presence of God.

At the end of five minutes of silent prayer, offer a prayer out loud, or invite the group to join in the "Our Father."

Trust Building and Sharing

Each person should reflect for several minutes and share the following with the rest of the group:

* This week, where did I perceive love in action?
* Where did I perceive the need for love to act?

If your group is quite large, ask members to form groups of five or six to share their responses to these questions.

Work Together

Review the material in the opening of this chapter together. Turn back to chapter 2 and review the polarity "Journey Out/Journey In." Where do you see your parish in this picture? Do you have a need to move toward the positive side of the journey out?

Planning for the Interviews

List the key players in your community. Write down names of town officials (the manager, mayor, city council members), the chamber of commerce director, recreation director, school principal, school nurse, chief of police, the pastor or rabbi of another significant congregation in town.

Decide which people are most important to interview, and then trim your list so that you have equal numbers of interviewers and interview subjects. Make interview assignments and agree on the date by which interviews will be completed, remembering that everyone is busy and some lead time may be required to schedule appointments.

How will you explain your reason for asking for the interview? Try role-playing a phone call:

> Ms. Town Manager, I'm _____ from First Church. We've under-taken a major strategic planning effort here, and one of our major considerations is our role in this community. We think you could help us to think about the needs in our community and how we might help meet them. I'd like to talk to you for about half an hour some-time before _____. What does your calendar look like?

Remind interviewers that you are asking just two questions:

1. What do you think are the most important needs in our community?
2. How do you think a congregation our size could help meet those needs?

Close the planning meeting with prayer. The person offering the prayer may want to pray specifically for courage and tact for the inter-viewers as they do their job.

Collating the Results

As before, tape newsprint to the wall and use markers to record the re-sults of the interviews as reports are made. Make sure every member can see all the data.

Ask each interviewer, How were you received when you went to conduct the interview? What was the tone of the interview? Then ask each interviewer to report on the answers to the two questions. When

everyone has finished, take some time to discuss what you see written on
the newsprint. Do you agree with what the interviewees said about your
community? Do you think the congregation sees the community in the
same light? Is there a difference in perception? Are some common
themes emerging? Cross out duplicate responses. Look at the remainder.
On a new sheet of paper, consolidate them into six to twelve statements.
Make sure everyone can see the list.

Almost certainly common themes have been popping out from the
interviews. One congregation in a declining mill town picked up these
comments from the people they interviewed.

What do you think are the most important needs in our community?

- Selectman: The economic climate affects families. Key problems
  include unemployment, underemployment, and low wages.
- Director of the chamber of commerce: We need to bring in more
  business to decrease the tax burden.
- Recreation director: There's a huge chasm between the haves and
  have-nots. People too easily accept lack of education.
- Pastor of a larger church: Our community suffers from what used to
  be called "social disease": poverty, homelessness, poor living condi-
  tions, alcoholism, chronic depression, lack of hope, poor self-image.
- School nurse: In our state, our county has the highest rate of teenage
  pregnancy and live births to people under eighteen, the lowest rate of
  prenatal care, a very high school dropout rate, and no alternative
  educational opportunities for pregnant teens. We also have a huge
  number of dysfunctional families, so teens lack parental support.
- Chief of police: We need to increase our tax base by attracting more
  industry and business.

These responses could be reduced to:

1. The financial problems in this town hurt the families living here.
2. Children particularly suffer from social problems and live in difficult
   family circumstances.
3. This town needs an infusion of economic growth.

How do you think our congregation could help meet those needs?

- Selectman: The church already helps by supporting the food pantry. Members could get more involved in community meetings or other community activities.
- Director of the chamber of commerce: I'd like to see First Church increase its visibility in town activities.
- Pastor of a larger church: A lot of these problems are too over-whelming for a single church, but First Church could work with other churches via the association of churches. I'd like to see early intervention and prevention programs for the most troubled families.
- School nurse: The church could help parents by running a mentor program for them. We need to work with parents!
- Chief of police: First Church could support the business element by working with them to bring new business to our community.
- Town manager: Members of congregations should attend town meetings.

Develop Interim Goal Statements

What are you to make of this range of analysis and advice? You have already distilled the first question to a handful of summaries. The responses to the second questions also need to be distilled. And then we need to do what we have done in previous chapters: turn the summary statements into interim goals.

Note the common threads running through the material distilled thus far. Make a list of up to six interim goals based on them. As an example, look once more at the mill town congregation above. What interim goal statements could they develop?

- Investigate programs run by the local association of churches.
- Through the association, participate in established programs or develop new ones to teach parenting skills and to promote family life, to help children, and to provide emergency housing.
- Increase the congregation's visibility at town events, such as town meetings.
- Seek ways to be involved in helping to improve the economy of the area.

Do not lose sight of the fact these interim goals will be added to other goals we have been accumulating. Interim goals are not final. Obviously no one parish could take on this much work and be focused enough to get even some of it done.

Next Steps

The strategic planning task force will meet with the congregation's board to prioritize goals. Confirm the date for this work day. Take these factors into consideration:

•   All members of the strategic planning task force, all board members, and the pastor or rabbi need to be present. This is going to be an important event in the life of the congregation!
•   Plan to work for at least six hours. Also allow for coffee breaks and lunch.
•   You will be taking all the goal statements that have been distilled from all work to date and determining the top six to eight priorities.

Closing

Close with sentence prayers, including:

•   prayers of thanksgiving for work done so far;
•   prayers for guidance to determine your congregation's role in meeting what may seem to be overwhelming needs around you.

CHAPTER 7

Prioritizing Goals

Even though you have been praying and listening to God throughout this planning process, now is the time to give discernment even more attention. This chapter describes two processes for following God's leading for the congregation. The entire list of goals under consideration should be distributed to the whole congregation at least a week before the fast begins. Members should be invited to call strategic planning task force or board members to talk about their discernment about the goals.

Fasting

Recall from our study of Acts 15 that the early Christians used to fast and pray when preparing to make tough decisions. If it suits the style of your congregation, call all members to a fast to draw attention to your corporate discernment. When we do not eat, we are reminded many times during the day that something is different here: "I'm hungry. Why am I doing this to myself? Oh, yes. Because our congregation leaders believe this time of decision making merits radical listening and praying."

Invite those who will be fasting to come to an orientation gathering at the beginning of the fast. We suggest meeting from 4:00 to 6:00 P.M. on a Monday. Present the guidelines for fasting provided in appendix A. People who have experienced fasting with a group know the power and sense of community that forms when people agree to fast and pray for an extended time. Even though those fasting might be together at the beginning of the fast only for a short time to receive guidance, all agree that "we are going to do this together." Those who fast always seem to develop a keen awareness of who else is going through the experience and how they are managing the process.

When the group meets again at the end of the fast to tell their stories, share the "demons they wrestled with," and so forth, participants always experience a sense of euphoria that "I actually was able to do this." Then comes a very special moment when all break the fast in silence by eating a piece of fruit. There is little else to compare it to. What a miracle solid food is! How we take it for granted. Some people are never the same after a lengthy fast, adopting the spiritual practice of "conscious eating."

All the while the fast is going on, those who participate are aware of the directions their congregation could pursue with this strategic plan. They are asked to discern the top goals in each growth area to which God is calling the congregation. They yearn to bring this discernment back to community, to share it with others, and to hear which priorities other members have chosen.

Several options are now presented for arriving at a set of priorities. First, the strategic planning task force and board could spend a day together setting the congregation's priorities. They listen carefully to one another. Each person lists his or her priorities on individual sheets of newsprint, and one by one the lists are reviewed. One ground rule is observed: No one is allowed to make negative comments about someone else's list. People offer only positive remarks about each selection.

The group is in search of the higher good. While listening to one another, they try to fashion new lists for themselves. They might choose to be alone for extended periods of silence, to return with new lists. Once again the same procedure is followed. People are encouraged to view only the positive side of each listed item. Eventually what should emerge is an affirmation of six to eight top goals, one or two in each of the four growth areas, that the congregation will pursue for the next few years.

(Congregations would be wise to engage in such discernment every four years. This should coincide with your clergyperson taking a three-month sabbatical. The sabbatical gives the pastor or rabbi the chance to acquire new skills needed to lead the congregation in a specific direction. More important, clergy need a periodic break to regain their vitality and enthusiasm for the Gospel, so they can hit the ground running when the congregation begins implementing a new strategic plan.)

An Alternate Process

If the process recommended above does not produce the desired results
—or if it does not suit your style as a congregation—use the process
described here.

What Should Happen

- Work with the twenty to thirty interim goal statements distilled from
  all work to date.
- As a congregation, determine the top one or two goals in each of the
  four growth areas.
- Present these goals to the congregation as a whole for its endorsement. (This procedure is described in chapter seven.)

Why It Should Happen

- No congregation, regardless of size, can work on more than six to
  eight major goals at once.
- Without a focus, the body of believers becomes confused (and probably annoyed with the leaders).

How It Might Be Done

This task is easier for a small group, in this case the strategic planning
task force and the board, to grasp and accomplish. It might be too cum-
bersome for a large group (such as the whole congregation, unless the
congregation is a family-size church).

At this stage, plan to work within each of the four growth areas, one
at a time. All goals accumulated up to this point should be categorized
under these four headings.

- Growth area 1: *strengths* to build on
- Growth area 2: *dysfunction* in our congregational life that needs to be
  fixed

- Growth area 3: *mission* to our communities
- Growth area 4: *aspirations* for the next four years

If there are duplicate interim goals, consolidate them into single statements ahead of time. Working with one growth area at a time, number all
the interim goals for that area and print them on an 8-1/2 x 11 sheet of
paper. Then make a copy of the sheet for each participant. You will also
need a pad of newsprint and an easel. The task is for each participant to
divide the goals for each growth area into thirds—one-third top-rated,
one-third middle-rated, and one-third bottom-rated goals. Participants
should put a T, M, or B next to each goal. If the number of goals within
a growth area is not evenly divisible by three, the group should determine how the rankings are to be distributed within that area. If there are
seven goals in growth area 1, for example, the group might decide they
will choose two top, two middle, and three bottom goals.

If you are holding this event at the church, make sure your group will
not be disturbed, and arrange to have someone provide coffee breaks and
meals, if necessary. The meeting room needs to be large enough so that
each person has adequate work space at a table. You also will need to
hang newsprint sheets on the walls, and people must be able to move
easily around the room.

Once housekeeping details have been tended to, lead the group in
this centering prayer.

Pray Together

Centering

Sit comfortably in your chair with your feet flat on the floor. Make
sure your chest, neck, and head are in a straight line. Close your
eyes. Allow your hands to lie loosely on your thighs. Do what you
need to do to relax your body. Because we often hold tension in our
faces, I especially invite you to relax your jaws; let your mouth drop
open slightly. Relax all the muscles around your mouth. Iron out all
the wrinkles in your forehead. Let your eyes be soft. Just imagine
they were couched in soft velvet. If anyone here to look at you right
now they would say, "The peace of God resides in this person. Look

at him or her. You can see it in the face." So, picture yourself being serene and calm. *(Pause.)* Hear yourself becoming calmer as your breathing becomes easier and deeper and your heart beat slows down. Feel yourself becoming more relaxed. *(Pause.)*

In this state of peace and calm, imagine you are floating in the sky above the church. You have x-ray vision, so you can see through the roof. You see yourself participating with other people in an activity. Watch yourself for a few moments. *(Pause.)* As you do this, think about what makes this place special for you. Who do you look forward to seeing when you come here? What are some of your favorite activities in this place? Which activities seem to feed your soul? *(Pause.)*

Think now about all the things that you have learned as a result of your participation in this congregation. Where has this congregation given you space and opportunity to grow and develop as a person? *(Pause.)* How has your relationship with the holy, Mysterious One, the one we call God, changed as a result of your participation in this congregation's life? How has your being part of this congregation helped you become a more loving, compassionate person? *(Pause.)*

Now, what would you miss most if some catastrophe struck this congregation? Think about never again being able to come to this place or to be with these people. What kind of a cavity would that create in your life? *(Pause.)*

Soon we will be participating in a discernment process to learn the next steps God wants us to take as a congregation. Before we proceed to that activity, review for yourself the things you want to see preserved as you think about this congregation's future. Without these, you would have difficulty remaining part of this community. Resolve to see that these continue to be strong features of this congregation. *(Pause.)*

In addition, reflect for a moment on the ways this congregation does not fully meet your personal and spiritual needs. Where are you generally left wanting as you participate in the life of this congregation? What things would you like to see in place? What things would make this place even more attractive for you? *(Pause.)* As you review the variety of goals that have emerged to this point in this planning process, which ones come closest to meeting these needs for you personally? *(Pause.)*

I invite you now to recall passages in the Book of Acts where the apostles had to meet and make some decisions about the shape the Jesus movement was taking. See if you can put yourself in their place. They must have felt a great responsibility to make the right decisions about the emerging church, knowing that their decisions might either make or break this evolving movement. Their leader had left them. They were on their own. Jesus had promised them the guidance of the Holy Spirit at times like this. Visualize them listening to the Spirit. Get some sense of the quality of their prayer life. Do you suppose they did spent time in silence simply listening to God? *(Pause.)*

Now in this silence, listen for whatever message God might have for you as you face decisions related to the future of this church. *(Allow several minutes of silence.)*

Eventually the apostles had to stop praying and get down to the business of deciding what was best for the church. That time has come for us as well. Take a moment and focus on your breathing. Be sure you are breathing easily, calmly, and deeply. *(Pause.)* Do a quick body scan and see if you have accumulated any tension during this exercise. Do what you need to do to relax your body again. Be sure you are grounded in grace. Remind yourself that you live by this total, unconditional, positive regard. When you are relaxed, slowly open your eyes, and we will continue with this discernment process.

Working with Scripture

Jesus operated his ministry with clear goals. Indeed, one overriding goal seemed to dominate his thinking and movements.

Read Luke 13:31-33. Then discuss these two questions:

• What was that overarching goal? (Feel free to examine the context of these verses in Luke.)
• Why is it important for us to know where we are headed?

(Limit the centering prayer and Bible study to thirty minutes total.)

Trust Building and Sharing

Ask everyone to take a few minutes to reflect on these two questions. Ask participants to share their responses with the entire group. If your group is too large, ask group members to form groups of five or six and to share their responses in their small groups:

What I like about what we are doing is _____.
What concerns me about what we are doing is _____.

Work Together

Clarifying the Goals

The first step in a discernment process is for everyone to have a clear perception of the options before them. In this case, all the interim goals should be laid before the participants. Allow time for questions and comments, and for people to add a goal or two to the list. People need to know they are free—even at this point—to add, subtract, or combine goals. Allow at least an hour for this clarifying activity. Be sure at the end of this step that everyone has identical sheets of interim goals. If goals have been added, each participant needs to write those new goals on the sheet for that growth area.

One congregation in the Washington, D.C., area began its work with these interim goals:

Growth area 1: **Strengths** *to build on*

(Which goals are so important to you that if they were not true of this congregation, you would not want to be a part of it?)

1. Create ways to show more effectively our openness to and acceptance of all who worship with us.
2. Implement ways to care more for children and each other in our congregation.
3. Declare publicly that we are and seek to be in practice a church that

truly welcomes and incorporates into our fellowship all people, regardless of race, sexual orientation, or spiritual beliefs.
4. Grow in our willingness to follow God's direction for us, and seek
    ways to act on that direction.
5. Develop further our emphasis on the important role lay people play
    in our worship services.
6. Strive to build on our view that the pastor is one leader among many
    leaders in our church, and to improve the way all our leaders work
    together.
7. Continue to emphasize that there must not be a codependent relation
    ship between the pastor and the church, and that every member is a
    minister.

Growth area 2: **Dysfunction** *in our congregational life that needs to be fixed*

(Which of these goals, if they were not implemented, would make you
seriously consider looking for another church?)

1. Discover and implement structures whereby we can learn to "put our
    cards on the table" and communicate openly about our needs and
    wants within the church.
2. Learn to focus energy outside ourselves by helping others.
3. Learn to disagree with each other, yet maintain trust in the integrity
    of others. As part of this, we will learn to fight quickly and fairly at
    the same time as we continue to care for one another.
4. Develop greater clarity about the structures of authority and respon-
    sibility in the church, so that individual roles and duties are under
    stood and respected so that the general quality of leadership is
    enhanced.
5. Become clearer about the role of the deacons within the church and
    how they are integral to our outreach to the congregation.
6. Overcome our survival mentality by learning to talk openly and
    honest about money and the spiritual nature of our relationship to it.

Growth area 3: **Mission** *to our communities*

(To which mission or ministry do you believe God is calling you?)

1. Form ourselves into mission groups, with each group choosing its own outreach projects. The following are possible projects:
   a. Support children in difficult circumstances.
   b. Recruit adults to serve as surrogate grandparents for children on the school's Grandparents Day (Friday before Mother's Day).
   c. Help find a doctor for Lovettsville (one who will not charge the indigent for services).
   d. Adopt elderly people who need help to stay in their own homes.
   e. Provide rides for seniors to Thursday luncheons at Lovettsville Community Center.
   f. Participate in Loudoun Volunteer Caregivers.
   g. Other options as suggested
2. Create effective ways to affirm and support each other in our individual ministries.

Growth area 4: **Aspirations** *for the next four years*

(Which of these goals, if any, do you believe match God's hopes and dreams for our church?)

1. Publicize to our communities who we are as St. James United Church of Christ and what distinguishes us from many other churches.
2. Publish and distribute a newsletter about St. James to the Loudoun County and Brunswick areas.
3. Develop a plan to double our size in four years (from average worship attendance of 35 to an average of 70).
4. Adopt a new hymnal for worship.
5. Improve the appearance of our sanctuary by painting it and rearranging the pews to enhance our sense of oneness and involvement in worship.
6. Provide new space for the Sunday school, perhaps by reclaiming the parsonage for education space.
7. Develop new approaches to deal more positively with money issues.
8. Encourage all members to adopt the four forms of spiritual health:
   a. Private prayer
   b. Membership in a small group

    c.   Sunday worship

    d.   Service to others

9.   Create opportunities for people to gather in groups to deal with life tasks and to grow spiritually.

Discernment

The second step is individual discernment. Set aside no less than ninety minutes for individuals to find some alone space and to contemplate the goals proposed for their congregation. Some people might want to go into the sanctuary of the church and simply spend some quiet prayer time there. Some might want to go for a walk.

St. Francis de Sales, a seventeenth-century French priest, bishop, and spiritual director, affirmed that loving God also means loving neighbor, and that the devout life is not one only of prayer and piety but also one of charity and service. He described this method for knowing God's will:

> [I]n matters of importance we are to use a great humility, and not to think that we can find God's will by force of examination and subtlety of discourse: but having implored the light of the Holy Spirit, applied our consideration to the seeking of God's good pleasure, taken the counsel of our director, and, perhaps of two or three other spiritual persons, we must resolve and determine in the name of God, and must not afterward question our choice, but devoutly, peacefully, and firmly keep and pursue it.
>
> (from *Treatise on the Love of God*, VIII, XIV)[1]

Francis's discernment method involves six steps, which you might outline for your group:

1.   The person must begin with an attitude of humility rooted in the awareness that it is God who reveals God's will to us and not we who deduce God's will by human effort alone.

2.   The believer must seek God's will within a context of prayer, especially prayer for the enlightenment of the Holy Spirit.

3. We must be predisposed to implement God's will, whatever it may be. The believer must have already decided to act according to God's good pleasure.

4. We should undertake this discernment communally by consulting with a spiritual guide or other trusted and spiritual persons. (This occurs with the large group later in the day.)

5. We must make a decision about the particular course of action God seems to be suggesting. Here, Francis especially warns against procrastination or excessive deliberation. Because we can trust in God's love and continued guidance, we need not feel anxious.

6. The believer should devoutly, peacefully, and firmly live out the decision she or he has made without worrying about the accuracy of the discernment. Francis teaches that normally decisions arrived at by discernment should not be changed. If God desires that a decision be reversed, God will make it eminently clear. Practically, a decision should be questioned only if the believer finds over a long period of time that the decision brings him or her neither personal tranquility nor to charitable service of others.

After a time of prayer, participants should study all the goals and within each growth area, label the goals T, M, or B. This might not be easy because all the goals might seem important. Remember, though, that giving a goal a bottom rating does not mean it is unimportant but that it is not as important as some of the others. Once participants have marked their sheets, they are ready for open-space time.

Dialogue

When everyone has finished, the facilitator invites all participants into an open space in the room. Hang three sheets of paper spaced well apart on the wall. Label the sheets "top," "middle," and "bottom." When the facilitator calls out the growth area and number of a specific goal, everyone stands under the sheet on the wall that shows how they rated that particular goal. At a glance, everyone will see how that goal has been rated. Allow people to "fuss" with each other about how they rated that particular goal. It is quite appropriate in this exercise for people to try to convince those standing under other signs to change their ratings of the goal. (If someone does change, remind the person to change the T, M, or B for that goal on the growth area sheet. The person must also change another goal ranking so that he or she still has the correct numbers of Ts, Ms, and Bs in each category.) If the group is locked in heated but productive discussion, allow more time for debate. The essential part of this method is the dialogue, not the actual voting results, so this is no time to call a premature halt to the discussion, particularly when there appears to be serious contention related to a specific goal.

The rationale for this method is that it gets down to basic positions quickly. You know where everyone stands on the issue because they are physically standing under the sheet that designates their view. Participants can more quickly get to the essence of the issue and possibly gain some resolution. But this is usually a fun time, done in good sport and prayerfully.

When it is clear that all arguments have been heard and everyone seems settled with their rating of that goal, call time and move on to the next goal. Follow this procedure until all the goals have been rated by the group. (This process might take a while, so you might want to take a break at some point.)

When you have completed this segment of the exercise, give the group a break while one or two volunteers help you rate each goal mathematically. Each top vote is worth three points; each middle vote, two points; and each bottom vote, one point. Work with one goal at a time like this:

number of top votes   _____ x 3 = _____
number of middle votes   _____ x 2 = _____
number of bottom votes   = _____
total score (add the above three figures) = _____

Example
Strengths

Goal 1   70 points
Goal 2   63 points

Goal 3 135 points
Goal 4   89 points
Goal 5   76 points
Goal 6 145 points
Goal 7   92 points

It is easy to see that the top two goals for the congregation in this growth area are 6 and 3. The other interim goals are important and will not be forgotten, but these are the top priorities. Some participants might be uneasy about the final outcome and prefer that the priorities were different. Allow discussion as people reflect on this selection of top goals for the congregation for the next four years. In particular, talk about (1) how many top priorities you want (we recommend no more than two in each growth area, and possibly only one each in growth areas two and three), and (2) whether the group wants to state a specific goal in a different way.

If a fair number of people sense that the priorities are not the right ones, allow room for the possibility that the process did not seem to produce the desired results. If some minor repair work gets things back on track, do that. If a number of people still have more serious problems with the outcome, agree to quit for the day and go home to pray about the plan. Agree that you will return at a specific date to re-examine the data produced by the congregation and to try again to select goals for the congregation. No single process can capture the Holy Spirit. The process of discernment might not work the same for each group.

Generally we have found that the end product surprises and delights the group and is cause for celebration. The Washington, D.C. area congregation mentioned above selected the following top priorities:

Growth area 1: **Strengths** *to build on*

1. We will declare publicly that we are a church that welcomes and incorporates into our fellowship all people, regardless of race, sexual orientation, or spiritual beliefs.
2. We will grow in our willingness to follow God's direction for us, and we will seek ways to act on that direction.

Growth area 2: **Dysfunction** *in our congregational life that needs to be fixed*

1. We will learn to communicate openly with one another about our needs and wants within the church, learning to disagree with each other while maintaining our mutual trust. We will learn to fight fairly while continuing to care for each other.
2. We will develop greater clarity about the structures of authority and responsibility in the church, so that individual roles and duties (like those of the deacons) are understood and respected and so that the general quality of leadership is enhanced. On an experimental basis, we will change the church council to seven members.

Growth area 3: **Mission** *to our communities*

1. We will support outreach projects dealing with
    a. Children in difficult circumstances;
    b. Care for the elderly, particularly through Loudoun Volunteer Caregivers.
2. We will create effective ways to affirm and support each other in our individual ministries, which might not be related to our church programs.

Growth area 4: **Aspirations** *for the next four years*

1. We will develop a plan to double our size in four years (from average worship attendance of 35 to an average of 70). The plan might include publicizing our congregation to the Loudoun County and Brunswick areas and providing new space for the Sunday school (perhaps by reclaiming the parsonage).
2. We will encourage all members to adopts the four forms of spiritual health:
    a. Private prayer
    b. Membership in a small group
    c. Sunday worship
    d. Service to others

Closing

Gather in a large circle and hold hands. Ask people to offer sentence prayers based on their feelings at this stage in the planning process. Do not be afraid of silence at the beginning. The prayers of the community will depend on how the discernment process has worked and will reflect the outcome. When everyone seems finished offering sentence prayers, close with the Lord's Prayer.

Next Steps

Depending on your polity, the board probably needs to vote to adopt these priorities. The vote could take place immediately following this meeting or at the board's next regular meeting (although momentum might be lost if the vote is delayed). Again depending on your polity, the congregation might also need to vote to adopt these priorities. This could come naturally at the last meeting in this process, when the plan is presented to the entire congregation.

Confirm the date for the congregational meeting. As you head toward that meeting, the primary need is for good communication with the congregation. Use all means at your disposal:

- word of mouth (especially the mouths of the strategic planning task force and board members, who all worked so hard on this)
- congregational newsletter
- Sunday morning announcements and sermons
- continued posting of progress sheets on the strategic planning bulletin board you began earlier

CHAPTER 8

The Congregational Meeting

What Should Happen

- Members of the congregation endorse the goals developed by the strategic planning task force and board and adopted by the board after the all-day priority setting session.
- Members are given an opportunity to make a personal commitment to implementing the plan.

Even at this stage of the process, the board and task force need to be open to parts of the vision being reshaped. In a corporate discernment process, you want to include the insights of the people who carry the passion about their congregation. Furthermore, it would be foolhardy to present the plan as a "done deal" if you want members to support the plan in the future. To own it, members need to feel that you have taken their perspective on things seriously.

On the other hand, you do not want to be too quick to change the results of such a long-term effort. The governing board and the strategic planning task force have already considered in detail the ideas being proposed at the congregational meeting and have found some ideas lack substance, should not be pursued right now, or would not inspire faithful, effective ministry in the long haul. Board members and task force members need to be ready to give a full explanation for the decisions made and still be open for new input from congregation members.

There is a polarity here that needs to be managed. The polarity looks like this:

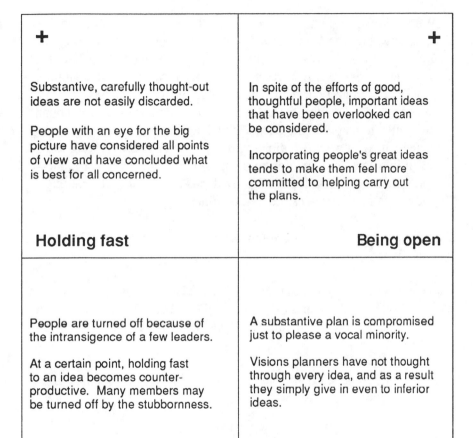

+

Substantive, carefully thought-out ideas are not easily discarded.

People with an eye for the big picture have considered all points of view and have concluded what is best for all concerned.

Holding fast

+

In spite of the efforts of good, thoughtful people, important ideas that have been overlooked can be considered.

Incorporating people's great ideas tends to make them feel more committed to helping carry out the plans.

Being open

People are turned off because of the intransigence of a few leaders.

At a certain point, holding fast to an idea becomes counter-productive. Many members may be turned off by the stubbornness.

-

A substantive plan is compromised just to please a vocal minority.

Visions planners have not thought through every idea, and as a result they simply give in even to inferior ideas.

-

Why It Should Happen

In the preface to this book, we, the authors, stated:

> We need to state right up front . . . that this is not yet another book
> on the need for the *leader* to have and impart a vision to the people.
> Quite the opposite. We are committed to a theology and methodol-
> ogy that places the entire *congregation* in the center of the visioning
> process. . . . Frankly, it would be simpler just to ask the pastor—or
> rector or vicar or rabbi—to come up with a plan, or to send the board
> away on a retreat to come back with a hastily concocted "mission
> statement." But we are dedicating this book to those who want to put
> effort into something harder, more substantial, and more workable—
> and something that will pay rich dividends in meaningful planning
> and congregational investment in the plan.

Both Hebrew and Christian Scriptures speak of the arrival of a New
Covenant wherein

- the Spirit is poured out on "all flesh" (Joel 2:28)
- "You are no longer strangers and aliens, but you are citizens with
  the saints and also members of the household of God"
  (Ephesians 2:19)

Recall also the Bible study in chapter 2 on Acts 15 ("It has seemed good
to the Holy Spirit and to us," v. 28).

How It Might Be Done

You need to publicize this event well. Be sure each of the presenters—
pastor, board members, and strategic planning task force members—
know what their parts will be. See that the room is set up so that everyone will be able to see and hear the presenters. If you decide to hold the
event in conjunction with a meal, make arrangements as needed.

Write each goal on a separate sheet of newsprint. The individual
newsprint sheets all need to be placed up front during the first part of the

congregational meeting. Later they will be moved to separate areas of the room. Attach sign-up sheets to each newsprint sheet.

If the pastor has not been at every meeting (as may be the case in large congregations), have occasional private meetings with the pastor. She or he must be committed to the strategic plan in order for it to have a real future. It has been said that the most effective power a pastor has is veto power. On the other hand, a pastor can exercise moral persuasion more than any other person in the congregation. (The possible exception to this is the family-sized church, with its powerful matriarchs and patriarchs. In such congregations, someone should meet privately with them, too. The matriarchs and patriarchs must have confidence in the process and its anticipated outcomes.)

Pray Together

Centering

Welcome the congregation and tend to housekeeping matters. Let them know you are delighted they have come and that their presence demonstrates their commitment to the congregation's health and future. Explain that you are going to share the results of a discernment and planning process that has engaged some of your key leaders for many months. Finally, let members know that none of the work will amount to much unless it includes the congregation's input and has their endorsement. Then invite members to join in this centering exercise.

> Let's spend some time getting ourselves centered and grounded in why we are doing all this in the first place. Sit comfortably in your chair, with your chest, neck, and head in a straight line, your feet flat on the floor, and your hands open loosely on your lap. Close your eyes. Let's take a minute to get in touch with our internal weather. Outside it is *(sunny, cool, whatever pertains)*. How is the weather inside you? Is the sun shining? Possibly a cloud or two? Maybe even a storm, depending upon what you have just been through? Take a moment to describe the weather inside you. *(Pause.)*
>
> What feelings do you bring specifically to this evening's session? You do not need to do anything about those feelings. Simply

note that they are there and that they will affect your participation here this evening. *(Pause.)* And now take a moment to check your self-image. How are you feeling about yourself right now? *(Pause.)*

Relax your body. Take a long deep breath, and when you exhale, feel yourself letting go. *(Pause.)* Take another deep breath, and when you exhale, feel yourself melting into your chair. *(Pause.)* All the muscles in your body are loose and limp and warm. It is the stress and strain of life that tends to shorten our lives. Yet our bodies, in their wisdom, begin to heal themselves when we relax. Let this be an evening of healing for all of us as we relax into the goodness of this community, and into the compassion of the God we seek to serve. *(Pause.)*

There is nothing we can do to earn God's grace, so we may as well relax into it. Think of your relaxed body as a faith statement. When you relax, you are in essence turning your life over to God. So picture yourself in the palm of God's hand with the sunshine of God's grace beaming down on you. Allow those beams of compassion to penetrate deeply into your body. Everywhere these beams touch, they relax, heal, and revitalize. *(Pause.)* Now allow this wonderful sense of God's peace to come over you. Don't try to understand it; just experience it. This is the peace that passes understanding. Become aware of how good it feels to do nothing except sit there, relax, and enjoy the peace of God. *(Allow at least two minutes of silence at this point.)* This is the peace the world cannot give. Millionaires can't buy it. It is ours to claim in faith, ours to enjoy.

Let's remind ourselves why we are trying to build a healthy congregation. Our congregation is a witness to the millions of people out there who are looking for this peace and don't know that's what they need. They try all sorts of ways to find this peace. Sometimes they end up in a dead-end alley. Sometimes they try things that turn out to be destructive. Sometimes they end up more confused than ever. This peace we know is ours to share. And you and I will be much more profound agents of this peace in a broken and a hurting world if we ourselves experience it more often. *(Pause.)*

Imagine people around you looking at you with great wonder, asking themselves how you can consistently claim such a peace in a world that is in constant turmoil. When they perceive this peace within you, they tend to listen when you speak. They think you know something they don't know—and you do. So let's covenant with each other to practice living in this peace as often as possible. We of all people can be at peace because we know nothing can hurt us. We may experience failure, illness, even death. But ultimately we know we belong to God and we will spend eternity with God. So we live in peace. *(Pause.)*

In a few moments, we are going to open our eyes. Take your time. We are in no hurry here this evening. When your breathing is easy, long, and deep; when your body is relaxed, slowly open your eyes and we will continue with the rest of the evening.

Working with Scripture

Ask for volunteers to read aloud Mark 12:38-40 and Mark 12:28-34. Explain that these passages both address the question, What's really important? Ask everyone present to form pairs and to identify for their partners one way this congregation, like the scribes, shows that it does not always know what's most important. Then ask everyone to identify one way this congregation, like Jesus, shows that it does know what's most important. Recalling Acts 15:28—It seemed good to the Holy Spirit and to us . . . (NIV)—pray for the guidance of the Holy Spirit this evening. *(Limit the centering prayer and Bible study to fifteen minutes total.)*

Work Together

Introducing the Top Priorities

The work session should begin with an introduction by the pastor or rabbi. He or she should assure members of his or her support for the outcome and express appreciation for the work already done and the focused mission work that will be done as a result of discernment and planning process.

The facilitator will probably want to take over here. Start with the top priority. Direct everyone's attention to the newsprint sheet with that goal written on it. A member of the board and a member of the strategic planning task force stand next to that sheet and, between them, read the goal aloud, explain it, and briefly explain why the planners think it is important. (It is best if they decide ahead of time who will do what.) They then field questions from the congregation. Repeat this process for each goal. It should take you close to an hour to introduce the goals and to field questions and comments. This will constitute the first half of the evening.

Making Commitments

During the second half of the evening, those present are invited to respond to the goal that is of most interest to them. The goal sheets should be rehung throughout the room, and chairs should be arranged in a circle next to each goal. Two board or strategic planning task force members should be seated next to each goal. Everyone else is invited to take a seat in the circle next to the goal that interests them most. The board and task force members lead a discussion about that specific goal and help interested members decide what objectives they would like to see explored under that goal.

The simplest and possibly the most effective way to put the priorities into action is to build committees, task forces, or work groups around them. Each goal then becomes the charter for a work group. Chances are this model will produce a streamlined and easily understood format for organizing the congregation and preparing it to carry out its mission. In addition, because the board and congregation are organized around mission, this model tends to generate the excitement needed to move from maintenance to mission. Participants in the discussion groups around each goal should be invited to be part of the work group that implements that goal. (They can sign up on the sheets attached to the goal sheet.)

Obviously, people will respond differently to this process. Some will simply ask questions. Most will be willing to sign their name indicating interest in that area of mission. Some will state a specific task to which they would like to commit. Board and task force members should be sure to record this information, which will be indispensable for the upcoming implementation stage of the project. After the meeting is over, leave these goal and sign-up sheets posted for a week or two. Encourage those who missed the meeting to look over the priorities and indicate what interests them most.

Let everyone know goals are not implemented overnight. It takes months. Some groups will take off and fly almost immediately. Others will lie dormant, waiting for the right person to take responsibility for bringing together the pieces to make it happen. Your congregation will look like an airport, with some planes in the hangar, some at the gate taking on passengers, some on the runway, others waiting to take off, and still others climbing to 30,000 feet. Each plane is where it is "supposed" to be.

Preparing to Write the Mission Statement

While everyone is still seated in circles around goals statements, ask them to do one more brief activity. Give everyone one blank sheet of paper. Ask them to spend no more than five minutes completing the following two sentences:

1. Our congregation is _____. (Individuals are to list as many adjectives as they can think of to describe the congregation.)
2. Our church is striving to become _____. (Here they are to indicate where they think the congregation is headed. This should have some stretch to it; you are headed in this direction, but you are not there yet. These are your hopes and dreams for the congregation.)

These sheets should be collected for the person who will write the first draft of a mission statement.

Closing

Ask everyone to form a large circle, hold hands, and offer short prayers of thanksgiving. The pastor or rabbi may close with a blessing.

Next Steps

The last step is to write the mission statement. If the strategic planning task force elects to have someone from the congregation write the mission statement, the task force's only role is to support and act as a sounding board for that person.

Implementing the goals is up to the governing board. The reason for
including the governing board in the priority-setting day is to garner their
investment and support of the strategic plan. Yet governing boards often
already have a full plate of tasks to deal with. Therefore, although the
planning task force needs to trust the process and turn over the reigns to
the governing board, we have often found it helpful to have the task force
meet every six months for the next two years just to monitor progress on
the strategic plan. As they see the congregation's plan begin to unfold,
they can offer their support and praise. Often members of the planning
task force have volunteered to serve in a work group to help implement a
single goal.

One or two of the more difficult or controversial goals might falter at
some point in the following two years. At this point the strategic planning task force may intervene and challenge the governing board to complete what the work group had set out to do. When a complete strategic
plan has been developed, members of the governing board are not able
simply to choose those goals that appeal to them and drop the remainder.
The *whole* plan needs to be implemented. The intervention of strategic
planning task force members can be the impetus to jump start goals that
have yet to really get off the ground.

Any worthwhile strategic plan is by nature a conflict resolution process. Sometimes, in fact, the reason a congregation does not pursue a
given goal is that it is surrounded by controversy. The decision to move
in that specific direction, however, likely came at some cost, and it
would be a shame, after going through the effort of choosing a particular
goal to have it falter because the governing board got nervous and began
dragging its feet. Decide how you're going to celebrate the completion of
each goal. Congregations rarely celebrate. They simply go on to deal
with the next problem. A specific plan to celebrate should be attached to
each goal. It's another way to communicate progress of the plan to both
active and inactive members.

CHAPTER 9

Developing a Mission Statement

A well-crafted mission statement is powerful. At the end of this planning process, a statement that captures the soul of your congregation and describes how your congregation is unique should emerge. The statement should state clearly and positively what it is you hope to become as a people of faith. A mission statement and a strategic plan tie together in the following ways:

- A mission statement outlines the broad purpose of the congregation and gives the strategic plan its context.
- The strategic plan is one concrete way the mission statement is to be implemented at this time.
- A mission statement is frequently used as a responsive reading in worship or before a meeting to capture the essence of the strategic plan and to state the plan in theological and spiritual terms. It thus reminds us where we as God's people in this congregation are heading at this time.

What Should Happen

- Pull together a precise summary of the congregation's strategic plan, plus other descriptors of the congregation, in a mission statement.
- Have one person write the first draft of a mission statement.
- Invite groups within the congregation to critique the first draft of the mission statement.
- Rewrite the mission statement as all interested parties offer their suggestions for improvement

Why It Should Happen

In many ways, the congregational mission statement is similar to personal affirmations. Research indicates that people who develop personal affirmations and consistently repeat them out loud are able over time to actualize these positive statements about themselves. In the same way, a congregation that affirms an identity through a mission statement will over time actualize that vision.

The actual process of developing a congregational mission statement can be as important as the final product. Congregational identity often is hard to get at, but congregations that are clear about their identity often are better able to realize their vision than those that are not. The vision statement helps the congregation stay focused on its vision.

Look at the following mission statement for an oil company. If oil companies can benefit from a mission statement, certainly a congregation can.

Phillips Petroleum Company

What we are . . .
An integrated petroleum company that explores for, produces, and upgrades oil and natural gas into petroleum products and chemicals for our customers.

Our mission is . . .

To be the top performer in each of our businesses in order to enhance the value of our shareholders' investment. We will utilize the teamwork of our people and the strength of our integrated operations to provide our customers with products that are high in quality and competitive in price.

We believe in . . .

- Maintaining a safe work environment
- Communicating openly and honestly

- Protecting the environment
- Treating one another with respect
- Giving equal opportunity to every employee
- Conducting ourselves ethically and responsibly
- Encouraging creativity, innovation, and teamwork
- Providing our customers with total quality in everything we do
- Contributing to the quality of life wherever we operate

Also examine the mission statement prepared by Trinity Lutheran Church and printed at the end of this chapter.

How It Might Be Done

The strategic planning task force needs to decide who is going to write the first draft of a mission statement. It is rarely a good idea for a group of people to try to write something. If they decide no one in their group has either the motivation or the ability to write a mission statement, they should then try to select someone with these gifts from the congregation.

They should ask the person if he or she would be willing to stay with the process through four revisions until a final draft is adopted. After each draft, the statement will go to another group in the congregation for review, thereby involving as many people as possible. The more times a mission statement is critiqued and rewritten by groups within the congregation, the better the statement will be, and more important, the more the congregation as a whole will own the final draft.

The strategic planning task force meets with the writer to explain what needs to be included in it. The key questions that need to be addressed are:

1. Identity: Who are we? What makes us unique?
2. Demographics: Who belongs to this congregation? Who belongs to this congregation's neighborhood?
3. Purpose: Why are we here?
   It is here that the final goals selected by the governing board and the congregation need to be included.
4. Style: How do we do things around here?
5. Shared values: What is important to us?

At the end of the last congregational meeting, members where asked to complete two sentences:

1. Our church is _____.
2. Our church is striving to become _____.

Individual responses were collected for the person who will write the mission statement. These responses provide another tool for the writer as she or he describes this congregation, its unique features, and where it is heading.

After the writer prepares a first draft of a mission statement, he or she meets with the strategic planning task force for a critique. The statement might be crafted as a responsive reading or a creedal statement and read out loud at this critique meeting or the next strategic planning task force meeting. Members of the task force could then talk about what they like and value about the first draft, and what they think needs to be added, deleted, or changed. The writer then prepares a second draft.

The second draft is presented at the next meeting of the governing board, perhaps as part of the opening devotion. The board then comments on the statement. The same draft could also be read and critiqued at every regular committee meeting that month. Committee members would affirm the parts of the statement they like and talk about what does not seem to fit or parts they do not like. At this point the writer prepares a third draft.

The third draft could be used as a responsive reading in corporate worship one Sunday morning. Members of the congregation could then write their comments on the back of the page. The comments could then be collected at the end of worship and given to the mission statement writer. By this time the statement should be nearing its final writing. The writer could prepare a fourth draft and ask that the governing board consider it as the final draft. The board might make some minor adjustments, but if they feel good about the draft, they could adopt it as the mission statement that will be used by the congregation for the next four years.

What makes writing a mission statement such a challenge is that everything needs to be stated in a few crisp words. The writer of the mission statement might actually develop three mission statements. The first could be about a page long; the second, a single paragraph; the third, a single sentence. Some congregations even fit the mission statement on a bumper sticker! A group in your congregation might enjoy the challenge of writing a sharp, pithy, or humorous slogan that people would proudly display on their cars. Writing a bumper sticker has to do with helping people feel proud of their congregation (rather than with communicating with the world), and this is a worthwhile activity.

Mission statements should be rewritten at least every four to five years. Congregations change over time and so should their mission statements. If a congregation develops a new strategic plan every four years, as we recommend, a new mission statement should be written along with each new set of strategic goals.

A well-crafted mission statement keeps congregational members focused as they go about making other congregational decisions. A statement can be read in a variety of settings, but we recommend that a mission statement be written in the form of a responsive reading and read in corporate worship at least once a quarter. Along with the other creeds you may recite, the mission statement summarizes what you believe about yourselves as a congregation and what you aspire to as a people of faith. The following is an example of a mission statement developed by a pastoral-sized congregation.

Trinity Lutheran Church
Mission Statement (First Draft)
(to be read responsively; L = left side, R = right side)

L: This day, we here at Trinity give glory and praise to God, Father, Son, and Holy Spirit, for the gifts of life and consciousness, and for the opportunity to worship with other baptized Christians.
R: We open ourselves once again to Christ's invitation to be drawn more deeply into a daily life of faith and compassion.
L: We enjoy God's peace as a gift of the Spirit, both now and in the hour of death.
R: We are a congregation of saints because of what and who God continues to shape us into becoming.
L: We believe that leadership is at the core of an effective congregation. We continually pray for our pastor, our church staff, and all the lay leaders who bring excellence to our congregational life.
R: We take seriously our name as evangelical Lutheran Christians, bearing witness to our faith to friends and family members.

L: We continually reach out to those who have not yet tasted the privilege of belonging to a caring, healing faith community.

R: We are grateful to the guests who visit with us this day, who honor us with their presence. We extend to them the right hand of fellowship.

L: We take seriously the power of prayer. We expect those for whom we pray to be transformed.

R: We believe that God heals when we participate in that ancient tradition of prayer and the laying on of hands.

L: We believe it is God's will that each of us experience health and wholeness—physically, emotionally, and spiritually.

R: We take seriously the education of our young and new Christians and provide them with the biblical, theological, and spiritual disciplines necessary for a life as Christ's ambassadors to a broken and hurting world.

L: We continually pray for the parents of children and provide them with growth opportunities to help them meet the challenges of raising children of faith, courage, and integrity,

R: We honor those in our midst who bring to us the wisdom, faith, and perspective of long years here on this earth. God has rewarded us greatly with the elders who have been given to us in this congregation.

L: We continually challenge all adults in our congregation to commit themselves to the central components of spiritual health, namely private prayer, study of Scripture with other Christians, and corporate worship. We continue our commitment to provide a variety of quality adult education opportunities.

R: We are a giving community, challenging one another to be more generous, moving toward giving away a tithe of our income.

L: In addition to supporting ministry to our own members, we pledge our support to the ministries of justice, truth, and mercy beyond our congregational walls.

R: We believe we cannot call ourselves disciples of Christ unless we in some way reach out to the poor, the hungry, the homeless, and the despairing.

L: We struggle to accomplish all of the above in grateful response to a loving God who has revealed himself to us in Jesus Christ.

R: We are baptized into the Christ, and daily we die and are resurrected to new life in him.

L: It is our desire to pattern our lives after his wisdom, his healing, his compassion, and his suffering.

All: To him be given all honor and glory, world without end. Amen.

Guidelines for Fasting

Roy M. Oswald

Fasting used to be a common spiritual discipline, dating back to Old
Testament times. The practice continued through the early church up to
the Reformation. During the Middle Ages, however, fasting fell into
some disfavor because it became linked with excessive ascetic practices
involving rigid regulations and extreme self-mortification. In the last
twenty years, however, there has been a renewed interest in the discipline
of fasting. Since the famous Swedish fast marches, some medical doctors
(Dr. Paavo O. Airola, *How to Stay Slim, Healthy and Young with Juice
Fasting*; Hereward Carrington Health Research, *Fasting for Health and
Long Life;* Herbert M. Sheldon, *Fasting Can Save Your Life*) have begun
advocating the practice of fasting for purely physical health reasons.
Some doctors (Dr. Jack Goldstein, *Triumph Over Disease by Fasting*)
even prescribe fasts for the cure of specific diseases and ailments.

Fasting and Spiritual Growth

Although it is recognized that fasting has many physical benefits, these
guidelines are about its primary spiritual purpose—as an aid to help us
focus on God. Like the prophetess Anna, we need to be worshipping
"with fasting and prayer" (Luke 2:37). The words *fasting, worship, and
prayer* belong together, as they did for the apostolic band at Antioch
(Acts 13:2-3).

Whether we are aware of it or not, at some level we all hunger for
God. If we are consistently satiated with food, it can be difficult to be in
touch with our deeper spiritual hunger. (For example, trying to meditate
on a full stomach is often difficult). On the other hand, we might also

stuff ourselves with food in a vain attempt to feed another kind of hunger, which cannot be satisfied with food.

The example of Jesus, who faced hunger and temptation in the desert, is an excellent model for us as we engage in the discipline of fasting (Matt. 4:1-4; Luke 4:1-4). When we are tempted to focus primarily on our physical existence, including eating, Jesus presents the way to a higher existence—to a life in which the central factor is not food but every word that comes from the mouth of God. Through fasting, we are confronted by our spiritual nature; the proclamation that "one does not live by bread alone" takes on a special force.

A sense of humility is central to fasting. In Psalm 69:10, David says, "I humbled my soul with fasting." Many Christians, when following the liturgical calendar, enter a period of fasting during Advent and Lent, recognized times for self-examination and penance. (During a seasonal fast, revelations about our own brokenness and estrangement from God need not be totally negative, however, because the good news of Christmas and Easter is quickly approaching. These festivals are truly feast days of celebration and rejoicing.)

Another purpose for fasting is to honor the deeper self—the self that is beyond our surface hunger and madness. As Jesus tells us, "The kingdom of God is within you" (Luke 17:21 KJV). When we fast, we are given another opportunity to discover our inner wisdom, our inner resource of love made possible through grace. Through prayer, meditation, or time set aside for quiet and rest, we are able to make the inward journey, possibly a journey into our own wildernesses to discern there the words from the mouth of God. Many people find that fasting enhances their ability to find quiet, reflective spaces in which to discover the incarnation of God in their own flesh. It can truly be an experience of joy and exhilaration.

In my personal experience, fasting is a time of self-discovery. Over the past three years, I have engaged in four- to six-day fasts, usually three or four times a year. I have experienced both wilderness and great joy during my longer fasts. During times of hunger and low energy, I often discover a darker side of myself. I have come upon my own desire to seek power, status, and bodily pleasure, rather than the will of God. At other times, a lighter, joyously energized self has emerged, full of praise and thanksgiving. There have been times of fasting when I was so energized and inspired that I would stay up most of the night to reflect and write.

Giving Your Fast a Focus

The underlying theme of fasting can vary from time to time. The themes of Advent and Lent suggest a fast focused on penance and self-examination. In Jewish tradition, the Day of Atonement is usually declared a fast day in honor of God's loving kindness in choosing and delivering his people. Before the trip back to Jerusalem, Ezra had the exiles fast and pray for safety on the bandit-infested road (Ezra 8:21-23). In response to Jonah's preaching, the entire city of Nineveh fasted.

Colleagues of mine, Gerald and Elizabeth Jud, fast one day a week for nuclear disarmament. Others, mindful that two-thirds of the world's people go to bed hungry every day, fast as an act of concern and identification, and give the money they save by not eating to a world hunger organization. One day in my therapy session, I was so struck by an insight into myself that I spontaneously observed a twenty-four-hour fast to help me remember and deepen that insight.

This has been my journey with fasting. Your fasting will be what it is. I encourage you to move through the difficulties and painful periods of fasting to the point where it will be whatever gift it will be for you. The following are some tips and guidelines to help you along the way.

Practical Tips on Fasting

A. People with relevant health problems or concerns should of course consult their physicians before embarking on any practice that might be problematic for their specific condition.

B. Eat only fresh fruit and vegetables during the twenty-four hours before beginning your fast. These foods help eliminate putrid or decaying materials in your digestive tract.

C. Juice fasting is recommended.
- Drink five or six glasses of juice, plus lots of water, in each twenty-four-hour period.

- Recommended juices include orange, grape, lemon, grapefruit, pineapple, pear, apple, and prune. The pectin in apple juice lingers in your stomach and will take away your hunger pangs for a couple of hours.

• Drink these juices in moderation: cranberry (it has corn syrup added to it); tomato and V8 (they usually have a lot of sodium in them).

• Drink *small* amounts of high sodium juice. We do need a little sodium—about 200 milligrams, or approximately 1/8 teaspoon—each day, especially when we are drinking lots of water.

• Avoid caffeine. Herb teas and hot water with a squeeze of lemon help get lots of liquid into your body. The fluids are important because they provide a way for your body to cleanse itself of toxins and other undesirable substances. Fasting can be a very cleansing process.

• Avoid alcohol of any kind.

D. Be prepared for some emotional land mines while fasting. Paying attention to these and tracking them often contributes to self-discovery during a fast.

E. If you feel like you miss out on table fellowship with family members or friends, simply take your glass of juice to the table and be part of the meal. Be in prayerful thanksgiving for the glass of juice that is your meal. Otherwise, use the extra time you would use in preparing for eating meals to be in prayer, take a nap, get a massage, take a quiet walk, or be in meditation.

F. Ending your fast properly is important. Begin eating solid food by first eating only fresh fruit. At your next meal, eat only fresh vegetables. These foods enter your system most easily and are most easily digested. Then add milk products and whole grains. Meat should be added last. Do not overeat. Eat slowly and chew food well. Allow the breaking of your fast to be meditative and reflective on the miracle of solid food becoming part of your body.

To Assist You in the Discernment Process

Centering Prayer

Make heavy use of centering prayer as you move into the final stages of this planning process. This is a discernment process and aids you in listening to God rather than only talking to God. This can be done any time in any place. It works best, however, when you are able to go to a special place that is conducive to prayer. Find a comfortable way to sit so your chest, neck, and head are in a straight line. Begin centering by repeating words or phrases that bring God to your mind, for example, "Be still and know that I am God," "I am—Thou art," "O God," "Kyrie Eleison," or "Lord, have mercy."

When you feel quieted and centered on God, stop the repetition of your centering phrase and imagine God asking you, What is it that you want from me? In the silence that follows, become more keenly aware of what exactly you want from God in this moment.

Once you have gained some clarity about what you want from God, move to silence and give God a chance to respond to your need, your longing, your request. Give yourself a nice chunk of time to "wait upon the Lord." Keep yourself focused on the presence of God with you in this moment.

After ten or twenty minutes of silence, move to the last part of this prayer form, which is to try to summarize your sense of God's response to you in this time. See if you can capture your sense of God's message to you in a word or phrase and begin repeating this word or phrase in time with your breath. This is the word of God for you at this time. Stay with the repetition of that word or phrase for another few minutes.

The more you practice this prayer form, the more attuned you can become to God's speaking to you "in the still small voice within." As you begin using this prayer form in connection with your planning process, you might ask more specifically about that plan and wait in silence to see if you have a message from God about which direction you and your congregation need to be heading in the next few years.

Journaling

Although this discipline is helpful during a fast, it stands alone in its
ability to assist us with spiritual insight. Journaling, rather than being a
recording of the past, is instead a process that assists in uncovering new
information from within. The process involves entering into a dialogue
with some important figure, usually a biblical figure, on a subject under
question. For example, members of your planning committee might take
thirty minutes to write out a dialogue with Jesus about your potential
plans. This is not a mind game. Our inner wisdom, which has accumulated a lot knowledge and insight about Jesus, gives Jesus a voice, and the
dialogue, once started, has a life of its own.
     The dialogue needs to be written out. Simply use an initial to signify
who you are, and note Jesus' response with the letter J. It works something like this:

R: Hi, Jesus, got a minute to talk over something?

J: Sure, Roy, what is on your mind?

R: Well, our congregation has just spent several months trying to discern
our future, and we have run up against some difficult choices.

J: That sounds familiar. I had a few of those in my lifetime as well.
Give me a sense of what your choices are.

R: Well, we know we need to grow spiritually in order to prepare for an
uncertain future, and we also want to grow in numbers. We can't decide
whether we can do the two simultaneously, or whether we need to focus
first on spiritual revitalization before we try to reach out to strangers and
newcomers?

J: Interesting dilemma. Here is my sense of how to proceed. You need
to...

     After the committee members write out such a dialogue, they can
come back together and either read aloud their dialogue or share a
summary of what they learned by doing the exercise.

This journaling process is yet another way to enter a discernment process and to test some ideas against some biblical and theological perspecitives.

Strength at the Center: A Congregational Health Inventory

(Developed by Roy M. Oswald, Senior Consultant, The Alban Institute, for the *Transforming Congregations Research Project*.)

Mission: To assist the chief decision-making bodies within a congregation to assess the congregation's health based on key elements needed for congregational growth and vitality. The goal is to develop a strategic plan that has the potential of moving the congregation toward great health, which in turn will lead to various kinds of growth.

Instructions: Allow time for each person engaged in the congregational assessment process to complete this survey. Their candid assessments enable the group to reach a consensus.

Once individuals have completed the inventory, the group doing the assessment comes together and reviews each section, reaching a consensus on a congregational rating of each item. When an item shows a wide range of individual ratings, time should be taken to hear each person's reasoning for their ratings. Then the group resolves the differences by reaching a consensus on the item.

Once consensus is reached on an item, the group can then select segments of the inventory that point to the greatest needs for transformation over the course of several years. At a future meeting, goals can be developed that might address low-rated areas that are central to the congregation's health and vitality. Rather than focusing completely on low ratings, however, be sure to emphasize the key strengths that also have emerged through this group assessment. Congregational goals should not only work to alleviate congregation problems, but should also ensure that key congregational strengths are emphasized in your mission statement and are assured prominence in the future life of the congregation. Healthy congregations lead with their strengths while also working to minimize the effects of their weaknesses.

Strength at the Center
A Congregational Health Inventory

Roy M. Oswald, The Alban Institute

When is a congregation an effective Christian community? According to the early church, these elements need to be present: (1) proclamation, (2) community development, and (3) service.

Segment A

Proclamation

Is this a "Good News" place?

1. Message: A strong message of grace, faith, hope, and love is proclaimed in the congregation week after week.

     1   2   3   4   5   6
Untrue   True

2. Music: The Good News is put into fine musical form on a regular basis.

     1   2   3   4   5   6
Untrue   True

3. Witness: Members share the Good News and a message of grace with one another.

     1   2   3   4   5   6
Untrue   True

4. Worship: Worship opportunities continually move people to awe, surrender, acceptance of grace, and praise.

     1   2   3   4   5   6
Untrue   True

5. Ministry: Members are consistently encouraged to identify their sense of God's call to daily ministry, and the congregation seeks ways to affirm and support members in this ministry.

1	2	3	4	5	6
Untrue					True

Add totals for segment A, **Proclamation** _____

Segment B

Community Development

Is this an inviting and supportive place?

6. Acceptance: I feel accepted and warmly supported in this congregation.

1	2	3	4	5	6
Untrue					True

7. Unity: There is a strong feeling of togetherness in this congregation.

1	2	3	4	5	6
Untrue					True

8. Conflict: Rather than gossip about someone they dislike or with whom they have a disagreement, members consistently will share their disagreements directly with those persons.

1	2	3	4	5	6
Untrue					True

9. Community Building: This congregation regularly provides social events where members can meet and get to know one another.

1	2	3	4	5	6
Untrue					True

10. Diversity: This congregation extends a warm welcome to a wide range of people (for example, people of different races, economic status, or sexual orientations; the physically challenged; the emotionally un-stable; people of different ages, marital status, weight, and political orientations).

1	2	3	4	5	6
Untrue					True

*Add totals for segment B, **Community Development** _____*

Segment C

Service

Does this place have energy for those outside the fellowship?

11. I delight in the way this congregation reaches out to those outside our membership who are in need, pain, or difficulty.

1	2	3	4	5	6
Untrue					True

12. This congregation gives me many opportunities to join with fellow congregants in service to a broken world.

1	2	3	4	5	6
Untrue					True

13. I am pleased with the benevolence giving of this congregation.

1	2	3	4	5	6
Untrue					True

14. In this congregation, we are consistently reminded that faith and action go hand in hand.

1	2	3	4	5	6
Untrue					True

15. The neighborhood surrounding our church facility is aware that we are concerned about their welfare.

        1   2   3   4   5   6
    Untrue   True

Add totals for segment C, Service _____

Segment D

Communicating the Tradition

Does this place have high quality ways of passing on its teachings?

16. I am pleased with the quality of our Sunday school.

        1   2   3   4   5   6
    Untrue   True

17. Our congregation offers at least one adult class of Bible study for every 100 members on our rolls.

        1   2   3   4   5   6
    Untrue   True

18. When an adult wants to become a baptized Christian in our congregation, we have a quality basic Christian instruction program of six to nine months that orients them well to Christian practice and belief.

        1   2   3   4   5   6
    Untrue   True

19. Our congregation consistently supports and encourages our members to engage in meaningful Christian rituals in their private or family lives (for example, offering private prayer, saying grace at meals, reading devotional material, engaging a spiritual direction, and the like).

        1   2   3   4   5   6
    Untrue   True

20. We make a point that we expect all our members to devote two hours to their congregation each Sabbath, one for worship and the other as part of an adult study group.

    1   2   3   4   5   6
Untrue   True

Add totals for segment D, **Communicating the Tradition** _____

Segment E

Assimilation of New Members

In Alban's research on congregations' assimilation of new members, we discovered that there are six stages a person goes though on the way from being an outsider to being an insider. These six stages are: (1) searching, (2) testing, (3) returning/affiliating, (4) joining, (5) going deeper, (6) being sent. We invite you to rate your congregation's effectiveness at each of these six stages.

Searching

21. Our members regularly invite their nonchurched friends and family members to attend our church with them.

    1   2   3   4   5   6
Untrue   True

22. Add two points to your score for each of the following items your congregation uses to attract new members.

_____ Bells, carillons
_____ A community newsletter
_____ Ads in a daily newspaper
_____ Radio/TV ads
_____ Attractive, inviting buildings
_____ 24-hour telephone messages for those who call after hours

_____ Attractive signs outside the church indicating times for worship
     and Sunday school
_____ Day care center, parochial school
_____ Ad in the Yellow Pages
_____ Other _____

23. Add two points for every nonparish community group that uses your facilities on a regular basis. _____

24. Add two points for every social ministry program that reaches out to people in need in the community.

_____ Meals on Wheels
_____ Soup kitchen
_____ Food pantry
_____ Clothing bank
_____ Senior citizen meal program
_____ Senior citizen social group
_____ Other _____

Testing

25. Our congregation easily recognizes visitors and has people who go out of their way to make visitors feel wanted and welcomed.

     1   2   3   4   5   6
  Untrue   True

26. It is rare that a visitor leaves our congregation without someone getting a name and address for follow-up purposes.

     1   2   3   4   5   6
  Untrue   True

Returning/Affiliating

27. Add to your score the number of points indicated if your congregation has the following:

_____ (10) Lay visitation teams that call on visitors within 48 hours
following the visitors' experience with our church
_____ (6) Lay visitation teams that call on visitors within a month
_____ (10) A staff member who considers calling on parish visitors a
high priority
_____ (6) A printed brochure or flyer that describes the nature of the
congregation, outlines parish programs, and introduces parish staff
_____ (4) A letter of welcome that is mailed to all visitors within a week
_____ (6) A clean, attractive nursery that is attended by friendly, competent people
_____ (10) A high quality Sunday school for all grades
_____ (6) An active youth or young adult program
_____ (10) A coordinator of lay volunteers who interview newcomers
when they begin to attend regularly to determine what groups they
might like to be part of
_____ (10) A variety of small groups (study, service, or decision-making)
that are open to receiving newcomers
_____ (10) Periodic, short orientation seminars for visitors

Joining

28. Our congregation requires all potential new members to attend new
member classes consisting of six sessions or more.

       1   2   3   4   5   6
    Untrue   True

29. Our congregation has a discipling program of six months or more for
people new to Christianity.

       1   2   3   4   5   6
    Untrue   True

30. Our congregation invites members to observe personal spiritual
disciplines on their own to support their spiritual growth.

       1   2   3   4   5   6
    Untrue   True

31. Our church receives new members at a worship service and celebrates their joining with a social event in their honor (for example, a congregational dinner or lunch with the pastor)

1	2	3	4	5	6
Untrue					True

Going Deeper

32. Our congregation consistently supports the idea that lay ministry is what Christians do in the world and community, and congregational activities are there to support this ministry.

1	2	3	4	5	6
Untrue					True

33. Our congregation has a written job description for every volunteer role in the congregation with clear time demands for each role.

1	2	3	4	5	6
Untrue					True

34. New members are interviewed regarding their motivations, skills, and growing edges to determine where they might like to contribute their time and talents.

1	2	3	4	5	6
Untrue					True

35. All congregational meetings end with a brief period of evaluation of both process and quality of decisions made, so that meetings can be improved.

1	2	3	4	5	6
Untrue					True

Being Sent

36. Our congregation consistently invites newcomers to work on New Member Ministries, especially to serve on lay visitation teams.

1	2	3	4	5	6
Untrue					True

Add totals for segment E, **Assimilation of New Members** _____

Segment F

Pastor/Parish Dynamics

One of the most important relationships within a congregation is that
between pastor and the parish. An effective clergyperson can do little in
a congregation if lay leaders do not work with their pastor in collegial
ways. Alternatively, a cadre of lay leaders who love their church and
want to see it grow can accomplish little if they do not have a pastor who
works with them because a pastor can bottleneck their efforts. What is
needed is a "good enough" collaborative relationship.

37. Our pastor enjoys broad support among the majority of people in this
congregation.

        1   2   3   4   5   6
     Untrue   True

38. At least once a year our pastor and chief decision-making body
engage in a mutual evaluation process.

        1   2   3   4   5   6
     Untrue   True

39. At least once every four years the entire congregation engages in a
ministry evaluation process (an evaluation of the entire ministry of the
parish, not just of the pastor).

        1   2   3   4   5   6
     Untrue   True

40. In addition to vacation, our pastor is encouraged to take two weeks of
continuing education a year and is supported in this with a budget of at
least $1,500.

        1   2   3   4   5   6
     Untrue   True

41. Once every four years our pastor in encouraged to take a three-month sabbatical, in addition to vacation, for the sake of personal and professional renewal and growth.

        1   2   3   4   5   6
     Untrue   True

42. When conflict arises between our pastor and individuals or a specific group of people, we are open to calling in an outside consultant to mediate differences.

        1   2   3   4   5   6
     Untrue   True

43. At least once a year, the role of our clergy is reviewed, with role negotiations taking place between our clergy and our chief decision-making body.

        1   2   3   4   5   6
     Untrue   True

*Add totals for segment F, **Pastor/Parish Dynamics** _____*

Segment G

Congregational Vision

Where there is no vision, the people perish. (Proverbs 29:18 KJV)

44. At least every four years our congregation engages in a strategic planning process that involves the entire congregation at certain points.

        1   2   3   4   5   6
     Untrue   True

45. A mission statement reflecting these goals plus the key strengths of the congregation is developed and used by the congregation on a regular basis (for example, as a responsive reading during worship, as a reading

before congregational meetings, and the like).

    1   2   3   4   5   6
Untrue   True

46. An annual stewardship program that involves contacting every member challenges members to support the congregation's vision as well as ongoing ministry opportunities.

    1   2   3   4   5   6
Untrue   True

*Add totals for segment G, **Congregational Vision** _____*

Segment H

Leadership

Without leadership, all of the above go nowhere.

47. Our congregation responds well to the leadership style of our clergy.

    1   2   3   4   5   6
Untrue   True

48. Our congregation enjoys the commitment and energy of lay people, in addition to clergy, with strong leadership skills.

    1   2   3   4   5   6
Untrue   True

49. The key power people in the congregation are supportive of our clergy and key lay leaders.

    1   2   3   4   5   6
Untrue   True

50. Our congregation continues to identify people with leadership potential and gives them both training and leadership opportunities to

further develop their skills.

1	2	3	4	5	6
Untrue					True

51. Our congregation monitors for burnout among our lay leaders to ensure that their energy and commitment to their roles remain high.

1	2	3	4	5	6
Untrue					True

*Add totals for segment H, **Leadership*** _____

Transfer total for each segment

A. Proclamation _____
B. Community Development _____
C. Service _____
D. Communicating the Tradition _____
E. Assimilation of New Members _____
F. Pastor/Parish Dynamics _____
G. Congregational Vision _____
H. Leadership _____
Total _____

Scoring

Corporate congregations (350+ average Sunday attendance)
Program congregations (150-350 average Sunday attendance)
Pastoral congregations (50-150 average Sunday attendance)
Family congregations (0-50 average Sunday attendance)

Good scores

Corporate congregations	270 or higher
Program congregations	240 or higher
Pastoral congregations	210 or higher
Family congregations	180 or higher

Fair scores

Corporate congregations	220 or higher
Program congregations	190 or higher
Pastoral congregations	160 or higher
Family congregations	130 or higher

Poor scores

Corporate congregations	180 or higher
Program congregations	150 or higher
Pastoral congregations	124 or higher
Family congregations	110 or higher

Centering Prayer

The practice of centering at the beginning of a gathering allows people to let go of all the baggage they brought with them to a session. Centering allows people to focus on themselves for a few minutes. Here's the general outline.

Ask people to close their eyes and look at the interior landscape of their lives. Encourage them to take deep breaths to help them relax physically. Explain that we relax best when the chest, neck, and head are in a straight line, our feet are flat on the floor, and our hands and arms fall loosely on the lap.

Encourage participants to loosen areas of tension in their bodies, and invite them to become aware of the predominant feelings rumbling around inside them. They need not do anything with those feelings but should just note that the feelings are there and affect their participation. Ask them to become aware of their self-image at the moment. Once again, do not ask them to change that self-image but simply to become aware of it.

After encouraging this heightened awareness of their bodies, feelings, and self-image, invite participants to become aware of any baggage they have brought with them to the session, maybe concerns heavy on their hearts or responsibilities left uncompleted. Because they can do nothing about these concerns at the moment, invite participants to package them up and send them to God. Suggest they take a few seconds to offer a silent prayer, unburdening themselves for the duration of the session. Invite them to give themselves the gift of being totally present and open to fellow participants and the content of the session.

Finally, invite them to try to view themselves through the eyes of God—with eyes of grace. Remind them that regardless of what feelings they have had rumbling about inside or their self-image, at this very moment God absolutely delights in their being. They are unique in the universe, and God holds their specialness close to His heart. In God's omnipresence, God has eyes only for them. Through their baptisms, they are connected to this God for eternity; there is absolutely nothing that can separate them from the love of God. Invite them to sit for a few moments and become aware of how good it feels to do absolutely nothing except enjoy the peace of God.

After a few minutes of silence, ask participants to become aware of where the group needs to be particularly open, in a listening stance, as you move to the agenda of the evening. Because the purpose of each meeting will be different, try to outline where you need to enter a discernment process, seeking the Spirit's guidance on the matters at hand.

Often it is helpful to offer meditations on sections of appropriate biblical passages, sometimes with opportunity for group discussion. Discussion should be kept brief and to the point. Some passages for meditation will come from the Hebrew Scriptures, others from the Christian Scriptures. The passages are meant to lend a broader, theological connection to the work being done.

In any event, do not give way to the temptation to skip over this time for personal spiritual growth in order to "get down to business." These times help people make the transition from their daily activities to the spiritual business of the session, and they pay rich dividends in the increased ability of participants to focus on the job at hand.

How to Minister Effectively in Family, Pastoral, Program, and Corporate Sized Churches

Part I: The Theory of Congregational Size

Clergy may be set up for failure when they move from effective work in one size congregation and begin a new pastorate in a different-sized congregation. If, for example, a pastor is thriving in a pastoral-sized congregation (50 to 150 average worship attendance) and then receives a call to a program-sized congregation (150 to 350 average worship attendance), that pastor will have to make a significant shift in style of ministry to be effective in this new congregation, too. Few middle judicatories pay attention to this transition in context of ministry; thus they fail to prepare their clergy adequately for a new style of pastoral leadership.

I would say it takes an unusually gifted pastor to shepherd a congregation from its birth to a corporate size. Few clergy have the flexibility required to accomplish all those necessary shifts in style. More is required than simply changing one's behavior. Because not only clergy but members too get stuck at each stage of growth, every time there is a shift in size clergy need to convince the congregation's leaders that a change in their behavior is warranted. Pastors of missions often take a congregation up to a certain size, only to reach a plateau at that level. The failure to grow is rarely the result of a conscious choice. Usually there are demographic factors that can be blamed. But at an unconscious level, the pastor has concluded that this is about as many people as she or he can handle. The congregation, also at an unconscious level, has colluded with that decision.

The theory of congregational size that I find most workable is Arlin Rothauge's, described in his booklet *Sizing Up a Congregation for New*

Member Ministry.[1] It was written to help congregations recognize the
different ways different sized churches assimilate new members. When a
theory is on target, however, it so accurately reflects reality that it can be
applied to other dimensions of a church's life and work. Rothauge's theory elicits consistent "ahas" from clergy who are reflecting on their transition from one size parish to another. Whether churches are growing or
downsizing, congregations hold on to deeply engrained assumptions
about what constitutes a dynamic church and what effective clergy do.
The inflexibility of these expectations is an important cause of clergy
malfunctioning.

Rothauge sets forth four basic congregational sizes. Each size requires a specific cluster of behaviors from its clergy. The average number of people attending weekly worship and the amount of money being
contributed regularly provide the most accurate gauge of church size.
Because membership rolls fluctuate wildly depending upon how frequently they are evaluated, they cannot provide an accurate measurement
of congregational size. Rothauge also holds that a church's size category
is a matter of attitude as much as numbers. I know one congregation that
averages 700 at Sunday worship and still functions on a pastoral model.
All the pastor did was preach on Sunday and visit people through the
week. The pastor's perception of his job burned him out and eventually
cost him his marriage and his ministry.

Here is a brief description of each of Rothauge's four sizes and my
understanding of what members expect of clergy in each size. As clergy
move into new congregations, they will profit from watching how a
congregation's expectations of its clergy, growing out of the church's
size and consequent dynamics, begin to be projected their way.

The Patriarchal/Matriarchal Church
(0 to 50 average worship attendance)

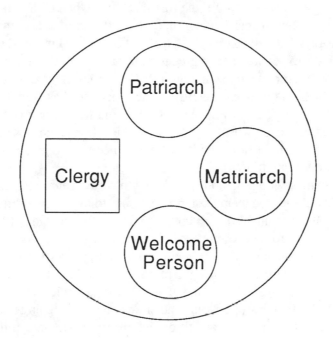

This small church can also be called a Family Church because it functions like a family, with appropriate parental figures. It is the patriarchs and matriarchs who control the church's leadership needs. What Family Churches want from clergy is pastoral care, period. For clergy to assume that they are also the chief executive officer and the resident religious authority is to make a serious blunder. The key role of the patriarch or matriarch is to see to it that clergy do not take the congregation off on a new direction of ministry. Clergy are to be the chaplains of this small family. When clergy don't understand this, they are likely to head into a direct confrontation with the parental figure. It is generally suicide for clergy to get caught in a showdown with the patriarchs and matriarchs within the first five years of their ministry in that place.

Clergy should not assume, however, that they have no role beyond pastoral care. In addition to providing quality worship and home and hospital visitation, clergy can play an important role as consultants to these patriarchs or matriarchs, befriending these parent figures and working alongside them, yet recognizing that when these parent figures decide against an idea, it's finished.

Clergy should watch out for the trap that is set when members complain to them about the patriarch or matriarch of the parish and encourage the pastor to take the parental figure on. Clergy who respond to such mutinous bids, expecting the congregation to back them in the showdown, betray their misunderstanding of the dynamics of small church ministry. The high turnover of clergy in these parishes has taught members that in the long run they have to live with old Mr. Schwartz who runs the feedmill, even when they don't like him. It is far too risky for members to get caught siding with pastors who come and go against their resident patriarch/matriarch.

Because these congregations usually cannot pay clergy an acceptable salary, many clergy see them as stepping stones to more rewarding opportunities. It is not unusual for a congregation of this size to list five successive clergy for every ten years of congregational life. As Lyle Schaller claims, the longer the pastorates, the more powerful clergy become. The shorter the pastorates, the more powerful laity become. These Family Churches have to develop one or two strong lay leaders at the center of their life. How else would they manage their ongoing existence through those long vacancies and through the short pastorates of the ineffective clergy who are often sent their way?

Loren Mead began his ministry in a Family Church in South Carolina. Later in his ministry he attended a clergy conference at which he discovered seven other clergy who had also started their ordained ministry in the same parish. As they talked, the seven clergy realized that, in view of the difference in their styles and the shortness of their tenures, the only way that parish survived was to take none of them seriously.

One of the worst places to go right out of seminary is to a Patriarchial/Matriarchial Church. Seminarians are up to their eyeballs in new theories and good ideas. They want to see if any of them work. Even though some of those good ideas might be the ticket to their small church's long-term growth and development, the church's openness to trying any of them is next to zero. Sometimes, through the sheer force of personal persuasion, a pastor will talk a congregation into trying a new program or two. Pretty soon parishioners find themselves coming to church events much more than they really need to or want to. As they begin then to withdraw their investment from these new programs, the clergy inevitably take it personally. Concluding that their gifts for ministry are not really valued in this place, they begin to seek a call elsewhere. On the way out of the church they give it a kick, letting the parish know in subtle ways that they are a miserable example of Christian community.

These small congregations have endured such recriminations for decades. The message they get from their executive is that they are a failure because they fail to grow while consuming inordinate amounts of time. Middle judicatories try to merge them, yoke them, close them—mostly to no avail. You can't kill these congregations with a stick. Large churches are far more vulnerable. An executive can place an incompetent pastor in a large church and lose 200 members in one year. Yet the same executive can throw incompetent clergy at Family Churches, leave them vacant for years, ignore them—all with little effect. The Family Church has learned to survive by relying on its own internal leadership.

These congregations need a pastor to stay and love them over at least ten years. This pastor would have to play by the rules and defer to the patriarch's or matriarch's leadership decisions for the first three to five years. At about year four or five, when the pastor does not leave, the congregation might find itself in somewhat of a crisis. At some level they are saying, "What do you mean, you are going to stay? No clergy stay here. There must be something the matter with you." Then the questioning might begin: "Can we really trust you? Naw! You are going to leave us like all the rest." In this questioning we can see the pain of these congregations. For a minute, let's put ourselves in their shoes and imagine an ordained leader walking out on us every few years, berating us on the way out. Would we invest in the next pastor who came to us? Not likely! It would be simply too painful. The Family Church might have invested in one five years ago, only to find that the pastor left just when things started to move. Basically these people have learned not to trust clergy who repeatedly abandon ship when they see no evidence of church growth.

I conclude that we need to refrain from sending these congregations seminary trained pastors. History demonstrates that these churches have not been served well by full-time, ordained clergy. The Episcopal Diocese of Nevada and the North Indiana Conference of the United Methodist Church are among judicatories experimenting with employing people indigenous to the communities, providing them with some basic training to give long-term pastoral care on a part-time basis. I believe long-term tentmaking ministries offer the best possibility for ministering to many of these Patriarchial/Matriarchial Churches.

If denominations and middle judicatories persist in placing newly ordained clergy in these parishes, they should do so only after laying out this theory for these clergy, helping them discover who indeed are the patriarchs and matriarchs of the parish, and suggesting some strategies for working with them. If these clergy find it simply too difficult to work with these parental figures, they need to let their executive know promptly. Rather than leaving these newly ordained clergy regretting they pursued ordained ministry in the first place, the executive should move them out of the Family Church.

The Pastoral Church
(50 to 150 average worship attendance)

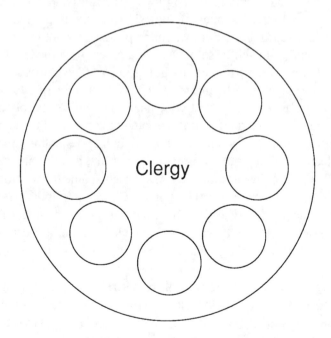

Clergy are usually at the center of a Pastoral Church. There are so many parental figures around that they need someone at the center to manage them. A leadership circle, made up of the pastor and a small cadre of lay leaders, replaces the patriarchs and matriarchs of the Family Church. The power and effectiveness of the leadership circle depends on good communication with the congregation and the ability of the pastor to delegate authority, assign responsibility, and recognize the accomplishments of others. Without such skill, the central pastoral function weakens the entire structure. The clergyperson becomes overworked, isolated, and exhausted, and may be attacked by other leaders. Finally the harmony of the fellowship circle degenerates.

A key feature of a Pastoral Church is that lay people experience having their spiritual needs met through their personal relationship with a seminary trained person. In a Pastoral Church, it would be rare for a Bible study or a prayer group to meet without the pastor. The pastor is also readily available in times of personal need and crisis. If a parishioner called the pastor and indicated that she needed some personal attention, the pastor would drop over to see her, probably that afternoon but certainly within the week—a qualitatively different experience from being told that the first available appointment to see the pastor in her office is two weeks from now. The time demands on the pastor of a Pastoral Church can become oppressive. Most members, however, will respond with loyalty to a reasonable level of attention and guidance from this central figure.

A second feature of the Pastoral Church is its sense of itself as a family where everyone knows everyone else. If you show up at church with your daughter Julie by the hand, everyone will greet you and Julie, too. When congregations begin to have 130 to 150 people coming every Sunday morning, they begin to get nervous. As Carl Dudley put it in *Unique Dynamics of the Small Church*,[2] they begin to feel "stuffed." Members wonder about the new faces that they don't know—people who don't know them. Are they beginning to lose the intimate fellowship they prize so highly?

Clergy also begin to feel stressed when they have more than 150 active members whom they try to know in depth. In fact, this is one of the reasons why clergy may keep the Pastoral Church from growing to the next larger size—the Program Church. If clergy have the idea firmly fixed in their heads that they are ineffective as a pastor unless they can relate in a profound and personal way with every member of the parish, then 150 active members (plus perhaps an even larger number of inactive members) is about all one person can manage.

There are some clergy who function at their highest level of effectiveness in the Pastoral Church. Given the different clusters of skills required for other sizes of congregations, some clergy should consider spending their entire career in this size congregation. Since the Pastoral Church can offer a pastor a decent salary, clergy do tend to stick around longer. If clergy can regard themselves as successful only when they become pastors of a large congregation, then 65 percent of mainline Protestant clergy are going to end their careers with feelings of failure. Two thirds of mainline Protestant congregations are either family- or pastoral-size churches.

Clergy with strong interpersonal skills fare well in the pastoral-size church. These clergy can feed continually on the richness of direct involvement in the highs and lows of people's lives. Clergy who enjoy being at the center of most activities also do well. There are lots of opportunities to preach and lead in worship and to serve as primary instructor in many class settings for both young and old. Outgoing, expressive people seem to be the best match for the style of ministry in the Pastoral Church. An open, interactive leadership style also seems to suit this size church best.

Growth in the Pastoral Church will depend mainly on the popularity and effectiveness of the pastor. People join the church because they like the interaction between pastor and people. When new people visit the congregation for the first time, it is likely to be the pastor who will make the follow-up house call.

When some congregations grow to the point where their pastor's time and energy is drawn off into many other activities and the one-on-one pastoral relationship begins to suffer, they may hire additional staff to handle these new functions so their pastor can once again have plenty of time for interpersonal caring. Unfortunately, this strategy will have limited success. To begin with, when you hire additional staff, you then have a multiple staff, which requires staff meetings, supervision, delegation, evaluation, and planning. These activities draw the pastor deeper into administration. Then, too, additional staff members tend to specialize in such things as Christian education, youth ministry, evangelism, or stewardship, which tends to add to the administrative role of the head of staff, rather than freeing up his or her time for pastoral care.

As we move to the next size congregation, notice the change in the diagram of the church's structure. Clergy consider a congregation's transition from pastoral- to program-size the most difficult. One can expect enormous resistance on the part of a Pastoral Church as it flirts with becoming a Program Church. Many churches make an unconscious choice not to make the transition and keep hovering around the level of 150 average worship attendance. The two treasured features of a Pastoral Church that will be lost if it becomes a Program Church are ready access to their religious leader and the feeling of oneness as a church family, where everyone knows everyone else and the church can function as a single cell community.

Two things prevent a congregation from making that transition. The first barrier is found in the clergy. When clergy hold on to a need to be connected in depth to all the active members, then they become the bottleneck to growth. The second barrier is found in the lay leaders who are unwilling to have many of their spiritual needs met by anyone except their ordained leader.

It is most helpful to put this theory up on newsprint before the chief decision-making body of the church and to ask them where they think they are as a parish. If they have been saying "yes, yes" to church growth with their lips, but "no, no" with their behavior, this theory can bring their resistance to the conscious level by pointing out the real costs they will face in growing. Churches tend to grow when parish leaders, fully aware of the cost of growth, make a conscious decision to proceed.

Without the backing of key lay leaders, the cost of moving from a pastoral- to a program-size church usually comes out of the pastor's hide. The parish may welcome the pastor's efforts in parish program development, while still expecting all the parish calling and one-on-one work to continue at the same high level as before. Burnout or a forced pastoral termination can often result.

The Program Church
(150 to 350 average worship attendance)

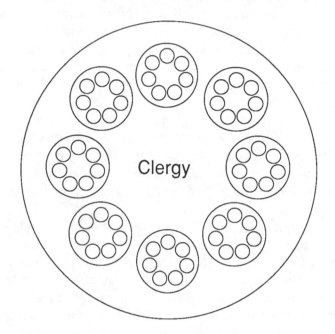

The Program Church grows out of the necessity for a high quality personal relationship with the pastor to be supplemented by other avenues of spiritual feeding. Programs must now begin to fulfill that role.

The well-functioning Program Church has many cells of activity, which are headed up by lay leaders. These lay leaders, in addition to providing structure and guidance for these cells, also take on some pastoral functions. The stewardship committee gathers for its monthly meeting, and the committee chair asks about a missing member, Mary Steward. Upon being told that Mary's daughter had to be taken to the hospital for an emergency operation, the chair will allow time for expressions of concern for Mary and her daughter. The chair may include both of them in an opening prayer. If the teacher of an adult class notices that someone in the class is feeling depressed, the teacher will often take the class member aside and inquire about his well-being. Even if the teacher eventually asks the pastor to intervene, the pastor has already gotten a lot of assistance from this lay leader.

Clergy are still at the center of the Program Church, but their role has shifted dramatically. Much of their time and attention must be spent in planning with other lay leaders to ensure the highest quality programs. The pastor must spend a lot of time recruiting people to head up these smaller ministries, training, supervising, and evaluating them, and seeing to it that their morale remains high. In essence the pastor must often step back from direct ministry with people to coordinate and support volunteers who offer this ministry. Unless the pastor gives high priority to their spiritual and pastoral needs, those programs will suffer.

To be sure, a member can expect a hospital or home call from the pastor when personal crisis or illness strikes. But members had better not expect this pastor to have a lot of time to drink coffee in people's kitchens. To see the pastor about a parish matter, they will probably have to make an appointment at the church office several weeks in advance.

When clergy move from a Pastoral Church to a Program Church, unless they are able to shift from a primarily interpersonal mode to a program planning and development mode, they will experience tension and difficulty in their new congregation. It is not that clergy will have no further need for their interpersonal skills. Far from it—they need to depend on them even more. But now those interpersonal skills will be placed at the service of the parish program.

Key skills for effective ministry in a Program Church begin with the ability to pull together the diverse elements of the parish into a mission statement. Helping the parish arrive at a consensus about its direction is essential. Next the pastor must be able to lead the parish toward attaining the goals that arise out of that consensus. In the Program Church, clergy need to be able to stand firm at the center of that consensus. To wilt in the face of opposition to this consensus will be seen as a lack of leadership ability. The Program Church pastor will also need to be able to motivate the most capable lay people in the parish to take on key components of the parish vision and to help make it become a reality. Developing the trust and loyalty of these parish leaders and ensuring their continued spiritual growth and development is another key part of the cluster of skills needed in the program-sized church.

For clergy who get their primary kicks out of direct pastoral care work, ministry in a Program Church may leave them with a chronic feeling of flatness and lack of fulfillment. Unless these clergy can learn to derive satisfaction from the work of pastoral administration, they should think twice about accepting a call to this size parish.

The Corporate Church
(350 or more average worship attendance)

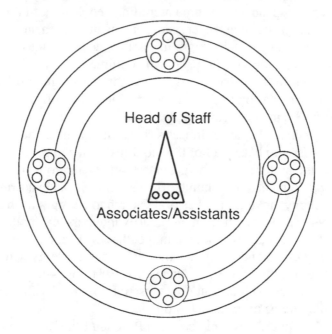

The quality of Sunday morning worship is the first thing you usually notice in a Corporate Church. Because these churches usually have abundant resources, they will usually have the finest organ and one of the best choirs in town. A lot of work goes into making Sunday worship a rich experience. The head of staff usually spends more time than other clergy preparing for preaching and worship leadership.

In very large corporate churches, the head of staff may not even remember the names of many parishioners. When members are in the hospital it is almost taken for granted that they will be visited by an associate or assistant pastor, rather than the senior pastor. Those who value highly the corporate church experience are willing to sacrifice a personal connection with the senior pastor in favor of the Corporate Church's variety and quality of program offerings.

Sometimes the head pastor is so prominent that the personage of the pastor acquires a legendary quality, especially in the course of a long pastorate. Few may know this person well, but the role does not require it.

The head pastor becomes a symbol of unity and stability in a very complicated congregational life.

The Corporate Church is distinguished from the Program Church by its complexity and diversity. The patriarchs and matriarchs return, but now they appear as the governing boards who formally, not just informally, control the church's life and future. Laity lead on many levels, and the Corporate Church provides opportunity to move up the ladder of influence.

Key to the success of the Corporate Church is the multiple staff and its ability to manage the diversity of its ministries in a collegial manner. Maintaining energy and momentum in a Corporate Church is very difficult when there is division within the parish staff. Any inability to work together harmoniously is especially evident during Sunday worship, where any tensions among the ordained leadership of the parish will manifest themselves in subtle ways.

It is at this point that clergy making the transition to the Corporate Church find themselves most vulnerable and unsupported. Our denominational systems do little to equip clergy to work collegially within a multiple staff. A three-day workshop on the multiple staff is a bare introduction. Leaders in industry with a master's degree in personnel management still make serious mistakes in hiring and developing leaders for the corporation. The head of staff of a Corporate Church learns to manage a multiple staff by trial and error. Sacrificing a few associate and assistant clergy on the altar of experience is the price the church pays for such lack of training.

For the most part we clergy are not taught to work collegially. In seminary we compete with one another for grades. Each of us retreats to his or her own cubicle to write term papers. There is little interaction in class. In seminary we don't really have to take each other seriously. This might change if, for example, a professor were to assign four seminarians to complete research on a church doctrine, write one paper, and receive a group grade. In that kind of learning atmosphere, we would have to take one another on and argue about our different theological perspectives and forms of piety. Unless our training can begin to equip us for collegial ministry, our seminaries will continue to turn out lone rangers who don't really have to work with other clergy until they get to the Corporate Church or the larger program church. By that time our patterns have been set.

The clergy who are called as heads of staff in a Corporate Churches

are usually multiskilled persons who have proven their skill in a great
variety of pastoral situations. Now, however, in a multiple staff, the senior minister will need to delegate some of those pastoral tasks to other
full-time staff members, who will inevitably want to do them differently.
Learning to allow these people to do things their own way is in itself a
major new demand.

Our research with the Myers-Briggs Type Indicator indicates that
congregations are best served when the multiple staff includes different
types. The more diverse the staff, the greater its ability to minister to a
diverse congregation. But this requirement for diversity makes multiple
staff functioning more complicated: the more diverse the staff, the harder
it is to understand and support one another's ministries.

Lay leaders are generally completely baffled by the inability of ordained people to work collegially. "If our religious leaders aren't able to
get along, what hope is there for this world?" they may wonder. Lay
leaders could help enormously by seeing to it that there is money in the
budget for regular consultative help for the staff. This help is not needed
only when tensions arise. Multiple staffs need to be meeting regularly
with an outside consultant to keep lines of communication open and
difficulties surfaced.

When the multiple staff is having fun working well together, this
graceful collegiality becomes contagious throughout the Corporate
Church. Lay people want to get on board and enjoy the camaraderie. The
parish has little difficulty filling the many volunteer jobs needed to run a
Corporate Church.

In addition to learning to manage a multiple staff, clergy making the
transition to head of staff need to hone their administrative skills. These
clergy are becoming chief executive officers of substantive operations.
Yet I would emphasize leadership skills over management skills. While
managers can manage the energy of a parish, leaders can *generate* energy. The Corporate Church needs leaders who know how to build momentum. Otherwise, even when managed well, these large churches run out
of gas and begin to decline.

In summary, the most difficult transitions in size are from Pastoral
to Program or, when downsizing, from Program to Pastoral. These are
two very different ways to be church. More is required than a theoretical
vision of the shift. We need to deal with the fact that a shift in size at this
level just doesn't feel right to people. Somewhere deep inside they begin
to sense that it doesn't feel like church anymore.

In order to help clergy and key lay leaders grasp the difference between these two sizes of churches, I have developed a simple questionnaire, which I call a differentiation exercise. Rather than have an audi-
ence simply circle answers to prepared questions, I like to send the As to
one side of the room and the Bs to the other side. You can see at a glance
where everyone stands on an issue, and the two groups can talk to each
other about their choices. Because the questions deal with choices clergy
need to make between two competing activities, I ask clergy to remain
silent until the lay leaders have answered. Then I ask clergy what their
personal preferences are on each question. I encourage clergy to choose
the activity they would most enjoy, rather than the one they believe
might claim a higher parish priority. Here are the questions:

Choice Points for Clergy

If your pastor has only limited time available in his/her week, would you
prefer that he/she chooses to

a) Do more visiting with shut-ins?
b) Put more time into sermon preparation?

a) Attend a wedding reception?
b) Go on a retreat with parish staff?

a) Call on prospective members?
b) Conduct a training session for church officers?

a) Visit a bereaved family?
b) Help two church officers resolve a conflict?

a) Make a hospital call on a fringe member?
b) Attend a continuing education event?

a) Engage in pastoral counseling with members?
b) Attend a planning event with officers?

a) Do more parish calling?
b) Recruit leaders for parish events?

a) Attend an activity with parish youth?
b) Critique a meeting with a church officer?

I have discovered several things by using this questionnaire:

1. Congregations may be program size, yet still require their clergy to attend to all the A activities. This is a perfect prescription for burnout. It can also lead to scapegoating clergy as "bad" because they don't accomplish all the tasks in the A column, while they are also expected to crank out quality programs for the parish.

2. Some clergy in Pastoral Churches should be focusing their energies and attention on the A activities. But because their background or training is in Program Churches, they continue to concentrate on the B activities or feel guilty because they aren't doing so.

3. Clergy and laity often disagree on priorities for clergy. This exercise often surfaces those differences quickly and makes role negotiation possible.

    Action research is needed on congregations that have successfully moved from one size to another. I envision several middle judicatories identifying congregations that have negotiated transitions—up or down. A team of consultants would spend several days with these congregations, trying to learn how they accomplished the transition. Their discoveries would provide material for a very helpful book. If you and your congregation have just come through one of these passages with flying colors, we here at Alban want to hear your story!

Part II: When Church Membership Declines

There are times when, no matter how capable, clergy cannot reverse the downward slide of congregational membership. The reasons may be simply demographic: At times certain areas of the country become depressed and begin to decline in population. In these areas, the older people may stay, but younger workers need to move elsewhere to find work.
    What then are the parish dynamics when a congregation becomes

smaller? What do clergy moving into those congregations need to pay attention to when the membership shrinks to the next size?

From Corporate to Program Size Church

The first thing these congregations are likely to lose is their ability to support a large multiple staff. The decision to cut down the full- and part-time church staff requires care. Areas of ministry that have been managed by the core staff will need to be turned over to church volunteers. All Corporate Churches depend on volunteers to do much of the work. Lay leaders who chair important committees have had the benefit of a staff person to confer with and to manage some of the administrative work of the committees. When staff is cut, these lay volunteers will need to take charge more fully, delegating the follow-through work that was previously carried out by a staff person.

Corporate Churches often have amassed some endowment funds. There will be a strong temptation to use some of these funds to support certain staff positions with the rationale that these staff members will help the church regain its former size. Such a strategy needs to be evaluated carefully. It may set the staff members up for failure because the church lacks the commitment, energy, and potential to make these former ministries flourish. Instead, new areas of ministry may need to be developed that do have vision and commitment behind them. If so, they will discover their own funding and not be dependent on endowment funds.

Deciding which staff positions to cut is difficult work, yet it must be done. It is easy to get caught between loyalties to faithful, hardworking staff members and a mission emphasis that might dictate retaining areas of ministry that do not correspond with present staff members' skills.

The place to start with all these decisions is to engage the core leadership of the parish in an assessment and planning process. I would recommend engaging an outside consultant and allowing plenty of time for this period of reflection, letting go, assessment, and goal setting. I recommend beginning with a historical reflection process, in which members can review the history of the parish and identify the strengths that have characterized the church's past and that need to be built into its future. Leaders can then confront directly some of the reasons for the decline in membership. Important grieving needs to take place during this process. To move too quickly to a mission statement would be to short-circuit an important developmental stage in moving to a new identity as a Program Church. People are going to have to let go of an image and an identity of being the biggest and the best. The Program Church has many strengths, yet the core leaders may not see those strengths because they have not adequately dealt with their grief about the death of "Old First Church."

From Program to Pastoral Church

Just as the movement from Pastoral Church to Program Church is experienced as the most difficult and traumatic, so moving from Program to Pastoral Church will present the congregation with a difficult transition. An identity needs to be relinquished. The wonderful team of volunteers that made everything happen in the church has largely disappeared. Many probably left because of burnout and sought a Corporate Church where they could rest and have their wounds healed.

There may be a faithful remaining core who will be tempted to try to pump the church up again by sheer commitment and energy. This faithful remnant needs to be spared the discouragement inherent in such an effort. Some serious downsizing needs to take place whereby all the separate program emphases of the parish are collapsed into a few small working groups. For example, rather than having separate committees for evangelism, stewardship, Christian education, property, social ministry, music and worship, these all may need to be combined into a committee on parish life, or these functions may need to be reclaimed by the vestry/session/council/consistory. One person in these decision-making groups can receive all the mail from the national church on one particular program emphasis. That person will occasionally head up a task force to accomplish certain goals in that area of ministry when such an effort is deemed important by the chief decision-making body.

The key issue in downsizing from Program to Pastoral Church is the responsible management of volunteer energies. A Program Church that shrinks to Pastoral size will surely burn out its lay leaders. Soon cynicism, disillusionment, and fatigue begins to permeate the whole parish. People will start serving on two or three committees just to keep them afloat. It's difficult to get the committees to do anything significant because everyone is simply too tired.

The downsizing strategy may include suspending all parish committees and programs and declaring sabbaticals for all parish leaders. Whatever activities occur in the parish during this time should be focused on the spiritual nurture and feeding of these parish leaders. The sabbatical period should end with a retreat or workshop at which members are invited to assess where God seems to be calling them to serve.

During or following this period of suspended activity, key leaders can be invited to an assessment and planning process. What is a parish identity that is both viable and energy-generating? Once members have gone through the process of grieving the loss of their former identity, they can discern a vision of the Pastoral Church that fills them with hope and excitement. Can this group once again find energy in doing things as a single unit, such as having parish dinners and activities in which everyone can participate? As they move from multiple services to one worship opportunity, can they begin to feel the advantages of having everyone worshipping together again?

Finally, can they begin to appreciate having more quality time with their pastor? Can they begin to allow their pastor to become the primary source of their spiritual feeding? What formerly was done in formal program settings can now be done informally around the edges. The pastor can once again know my teenage son personally rather than having to ensure that there is a youth group to minister to him. The pastor needs to let go of many administrative and program development tasks and begin to appear in people's lives in a variety of informal settings. Visiting people in their places of employment to experience the context of a person's lay ministry might be a good place to start. People will much more easily let go of some of their program needs when they begin to feel more cared for personally.

Moving From Pastoral to Family-Sized Church

This transition will be inaugurated by a congregation's discovery that it can no longer support a full-time ordained person. This is likely to occur when a pastor resigns, and in working things through with their middle judicatory officials, the church leaders become clear that they can no longer afford a pay package that will meet the minimum salary scale set by the denomination.

This discovery is often a traumatic point in the life of a parish. Members see inability to afford their own pastor as a sign of failure. For many of the older members, the loss is seen in no longer having a pastor to live in their parsonage. We should not underestimate the unconscious anxiety that is produced in the lives of many people when they realize they do not have a religious authority available to them around the clock in their community. They may rarely have taken advantage of the opportunity to call on the services of the person living in their parsonage, yet it was more the possibility than the actuality that was important to them.

One of the clear advantages of a congregation moving from a pastoral- to a family-sized church is that such an abnormally high percentage of their income does not now have to go into supporting a pastor. They may find they have some money to support other kinds of parish activities. The other advantage, which may come as a blessing in disguise, is that they need to get clear about what pastoral services are essential to them in order for them to function well as a religious community. That clarity has the effect of helping the parish leaders also become clear about the roles and responsibilities that will not be covered by a pastor and that need to be picked up by lay volunteers. Seen in a positive light, this clarity can open up opportunities for fulfilling ministries for some lay leaders.

True to its nature as a Patriarchial/Matriarchial Church, the parish needs to assume control of its own life, taking over all leadership functions, and delegating pastoral care ministries to clergy. The members need to stay focused on the direction of their parish and not allow it to be swayed by the ideas of clergy who have only a temporary investment in the parish.

From Family-Sized Church to Nonexistence

There have been congregations that, when confronted with the alternative of either living or dying, have made the conscious decision to die. In the process of dying well, they generated so much energy that they changed their minds. One UCC congregation in St. Louis hired an interim pastor who was to help them die well. That was eight years ago. They are a thriving congregation.

A Christian Church (Disciples of Christ) congregation in Bethesda, Maryland, voted two years ago to terminate its life, and they have effectively done so, merging their assets with a neighboring congregation. Their long-term pastor saw them through the closure and was himself awarded a sabbatical once the parish had closed. Their decision was quite deliberate, and even through they had endowment funds that could have kept them open, they choose instead to end with dignity and merge with a neighboring congregation.

The above two examples are anecdotes about congregation closures. I suspect there are more such examples. It would be helpful if someone would compile a variety of models from which congregations may choose. In this era of church decline I believe we need to get better at shutting down more quickly and effectively. There are some congregations that need and want to die. Dying well is qualitatively different from simply fading into oblivion. We need to learn how to help churches die well.

(Roy M. Oswald, *Action Information* May/June 1991.)

Norms: Every Church Has Them

Norms are largely unconscious for us most of the time. Our purpose in the evening of norm identification is to work together to make our norms conscious. If they are under the table (not in a sinister way), we are going to try to put them on top of the table with those we are already aware of. There we can look at them and analyze them. We can even decide what is healthy and worth keeping, and what we may want to jettison as unhealthy or unhelpful.

A parish is a type of family system. Its parts are unavoidably interconnected, and together these parts form a whole. It is vital that we think systemically about our congregations. No one person is "the cause of all the trouble around here." No pastor is "the reason we did so poorly then." All of us—all parts of our congregational system—think, feel, and act the way we do as a result or our interactions as members of this system.

Family systems therapists refer to "family strategies," which largely go unnoticed by outsiders and that frequently are unstated and not always understood by the participants themselves. Nonverbal exchange patterns between family members in particular represent subtle, coded transactions that may transmit family "rules." Norms are those unwritten psychological rules that govern the way any human community behaves. They are generally unconscious, especially for people who have been part of the community for a long time. People are not *trying* to keep "secrets" from one another. Norms simply are *by definition* unconscious and therefore unspoken.

At one church, the usual entrance is through the back door because that door is right off the parking lot. The official entrance, through the narthex, is large and inviting and leads right into the nave of a beautiful church. But the entrance people actually use leads into a dimly lit hall with five, shut black doors. "Everyone" knows those doors lead to important places (or a closet), but there is no way for a newcomer to know that. One norm is that "everyone" is expected to know where each door leads. Another norm is that people are expected to keep all the doors shut in the winter to conserve heat. All this makes sense to the initiated, but a newcomer feels like the character in "The Lady and the Tiger"!

The longer we live with our parish norms, the more unaware we become of their very existence. The norms become "just the way we do things around here." Newcomers are most cognizant of parish norms. The interesting thing is that the newcomers themselves come equipped with their own set of norms, which may have come from their last church home or the one where they grew up. At first newcomers expect your congregation's norms to be similar to those they are used to. When they discover the differences, they might feel surprised or sometimes even experience pain. Worse yet, they might feel anger or disgust. Their immediate—though unvoiced—question usually is, "Why do you do it that way?" You can learn a lot by interviewing your newcomers. They are the ones most able to tell you which norms make you attractive and which are a turn-off. Once you become aware of your norms, you can make an informed choice to change or alter destructive norms while enhancing and emphasizing the positive.

A large, wealthy, downtown church made just such a discovery about its norms for newcomers. This norm was at work: During the coffee hour, held in a large, well-appointed room with tables for four, it was perfectly all right for members to play catch-up with their friends while strangers stood alone on the sidelines, coffee cups in hand. People in the church had done this for years. It was almost like a "hazing" newcomers had to endure if they wanted to become members of the parish. For years this parish touted many members on the city's "who's who" list. When asked, newcomers said that to join the church you had to run the gauntlet of humiliation and embarrassment. At one time people had been willing to fight their way in because they wanted to belong to this prestigious church. Unfortunately, both the church's reputation and its membership had seriously declined in the past ten years. The norm that left newcomers standing on the sidelines was going to have to change if the church was going to have a run at reversing the trend.

You can find the roots of a parish's norms in its history. In the last all-parish event, "An Evening of Historical Reflection," you had the opportunity to review the history of your parish. By doing that, you laid the foundation for uncovering both the positive and negative norms at work in your congregation. Out of that exercise came prioritized meaning statements. Examine them again. They are probably beginning to look like goals. At the end of the norm identification process, you will have again the opportunity to develop goals that capitalize on your positive norms and that alter or minimize destructive norms.

The point is to work on goals that are primary, not secondary. Primary goals—and the norms that address them—have to do with the quality of your community religious life. Secondary goals and their spin-offs address the sort of issues you find in business plans or five-year plans: How much shall we raise the budget this year? Shall we repair the roof? Does the organ need repair or replacement?

Identifying Norms

The great temptation when identifying norms is to engage in a certain amount of denial. "We would never do *that!*" we protest. Actually, we might do that, and we would do well to make ourselves conscious of those things about ourselves—norms—that are destructive and constructive. Then we have a solid basis for helpful change.

Every parish has unwritten rules related to a number of groups of people or issues. Here are several typical categories:

• Children

> How are they viewed and treated?
> What behavior is expected of children and parents?
> What does our "adult space" say about our attitude toward them?
> What does our "child space" say about our attitude toward them?

• Men/Women

> In what ways are they treated the same?
> How are they treated differently?
> What behavior is expected of men that is different from that expected of women, and vice versa?
> What expectations are positive and what expectations are negative?

- Conflict

  How are differences of opinion dealt with or resolved?
  What confrontational behavior is expected?
  What topics are taboo?
  With whom may you disagree and with whom may you not disagree?

- Money

  How much money are people expected to give?
  How is money managed and spent?
  Which efforts have higher priority than others?
  Who gets to decide how money is spent?

- Treatment of Clergy

  How are clergy addressed?
  How well are they paid?
  What behavior is expected of them? of their families?
  When are they expected to be taken seriously and when not?
  How do congregants have a right to abuse them?

- Newcomers

  Who talks to them?
  What behavior is expected of them?
  What limits are placed on their power?
  To what extent are their foibles forgiven?
  Who is welcome here? (Do not fall into the trap of answering, "Everyone, of course!" All congregations are naturally and unconsciously more welcoming to some people than to others. A telling exercise is "Welcome Rating," pages 51-52 in Roy M. Oswald, *Making Your Church More Inviting, A Step-by-Step Guide for In-Church Training* [Washington, D.C.: The Alban Institute, 1993]).

Other matters for which your congregation might have norms include use of the building, timeliness, dress, language, and expectations of members.

NOTES

Chapter 1
1. Charles M. Olsen, *Transforming Church Boards into Communities of Spiritual Leaders* (Bethesda, Md.: The Alban Institute, 1995), 87-88.
2. Ibid. 91-92.

Chapter 2
1. Edwin H. Friedman, *Family Process in Church and Synagogue* (New York: The Guilford Press, 1985), 27.
2. The following material is based on Arlin J. Rothauge, *Reshaping a Congregation for a New Future* (New York: Episcopal Church Center, 1985), 11-14.
3. Ibid. 14.
4. For a seminal discussion of this concept, see Barry Johnson, *Polarity Management: Identifying and Managing Unsolvable Problems* (Amherst, Mass.: HRD Press, 1992).

Chapter 4
1. Peter Senge, *The Fifth Discipline: Strategies and Goals for Developing Learning Organizations* (New York: Doubleday, 1994).
2. From an evening of historical reflection, December 1994, at the Episcopal Church of the Epiphany, Newport, New Hampshire.

Chapter 5
1. From an evening of norm identification at the Episcopal Church of the Epiphany, Newport, New Hampshire.

Chapter 7

1. Richard J. Sweeney, "Discernment in the Spiritual Direction of St. Frances de Sales," *Review for Religious* 39 (Fall 1980).

Appendix D pt. 1

1. Arlin Rothauge, *Sizing Up a Congregation for New Member Ministry* (New York: The Episcopal Church Center, 1985). Write to: The Episcopal Church Center, 815 Second Avenue, New York, NY 10017.

2. Carl Dudley, *Unique Dynamics of the Small Church* (Washington, D.C.: The Alban Institute). Another helpful book is Lyle Schaller's *Looking in the Mirror* (Nashville: Abingdon Press, 1984).